T0129827

The Bird's Song

Linda Jean Santiago

Editor: Angelia Marie Kelly

Order this book online at www.trafford.com
or email orders@trafford.com

Most Trafford titles are also available at major online book retailers.

Printed in Victoria, BC, Canada.

ISBN: 978-1-4269-2483-5 (Soft)

Library of Congress Control Number: 2010901222

*Our mission is to efficiently provide the world's finest, most comprehensive
book publishing service, enabling every author to experience success.
To find out how to publish your book, your way, and have it available
worldwide, visit us online at www.trafford.com*

Trafford rev. 02/05/2010

North America & international
toll-free: 1 888 232 4444 (USA & Canada)
phone: 250 383 6864 ♦ fax: 812 355 4082

Dedication

To my Mother Shirley and Father Tom without you this book would not be possible. Also to Cheryl, Terri, Thomas, Tammy "The Phillips Family"

Acknowledgements

I would like to thank my mother for helping me with some of the stories in this book and thanks to my best friend Rafael Guzman for the encouragement you gave me during the making of this book from journals to book form. I would also like to thank my daughters Monica and Jessica for their support!

Chapter # 1

August 4, 1935, a baby boy was born barley alive. The day was hot in Montrose, Pennsylvania. The baby's mother thought that it was a good idea to wrap the baby in a blanket, put him in a cigar box and place him on the window sill just as placing him in an incubator.

The midwife told Anna, the baby's mother that he may not survive because he was not more than three pounds. Anna called for Floyd her husband to go and find the priest to have their baby blessed. As the sun went down Anna said to Floyd we have to name our little baby boy. Anna's brother Johnny came to the house for a visit, he loved his sister Anna and he wanted her to laugh, so to help dry her tears, Johnny spoke up and said your new baby looks just like the way I remember the story of little Tom Thumb! Anna laughed and said that he does look like what you could imagine him looking like. Then we shall call him Tom from this day forward. Floyd, Tom's father agreed. Floyd said I would like him to have my name though we could call him Tom for short. Than Anna said we could name him Floyd Matthew (Tom) Phillips Jr.

The very next day the priest came to see Tom. As the priest entered the Phillips family home he noticed that Tom was in a cigar box on the window sill. The priest was stunned to see such a sight. A baby sleeping in a cigar box on a window sill, he replied! The priest then lifted Tom out of his makeshift crib and Tom's mother began to cry. Please bless my son and ask God to do as he plans to do with him. I pray that he lives to be a man! Anna said with a faint smile.

He is feeding and sleeping like a healthy baby. The priest began to pray, Dear God in heaven

Bless this small and frail child, keep this family safe from the trials that they face. Give them the strength to carry on no matter what thy will is. In your blessed name I pray. The priest christened Tom with the name of Floyd Matthew Francis Phillips Jr. which would be his legal name. He then laid Tom in his makeshift crib trying not to wake up the tiny baby. As the priest turned to leave, Tom let out a small little cry. The priest was surprised because the baby was sleeping the entire time.

Anna said that we must be excused now because Tom wanted to be nursed. They were all so excited that the baby wanted to eat because he seemed so frail. The priest said I must go now. Take care of your little son. I will continue to pray for you and your little ones.

Anna asked Floyd to go to town and bring home Tom's brother and sister (Jerry) and (Josephine) from Aunt Peony's house. Floyd left for town with Anna's brother Johnny. Floyd and Anna lived on road 581 also known as Rafferty Road, which was out in the country near Anna's parents Thomas and Annie who were in Ireland. They were not in Montrose when Tom was born and his brother and sister had to go to Anna's brother and sister-in-laws house to stay for a while.

Floyd returned without the children. Anna asked as he walked into the house, where are the kids? I'm sorry honey; we all thought that you needed time to be with our new baby, considering the circumstances. Anna sighed; I guess that I can wait a little longer to see them.

As the days passed, Tom got stronger and he grew like a weed. Anna called her sister-in-law to check up on her other two children telling them I miss you both. Peony told Anna that the children were missing her and they wanted to go home to her. Anna replied that it was time for them to come home to meet their brother. Tom was one month old by this time.

About an hour later Anna heard a car come up the driveway. As she suspected it was Peony with her two children in tow. Tom was still sleeping in the cigar box on the window sill. As the children were walking they were screaming Ma Ma! Who is that baby on the window sill? Anna said that is your new brother Tom!

He looks like a baby doll Josephine replied! At that moment Tom woke up and was crying. Anna picked him up to comfort him and he became quiet. Josephine said Mama, he looks like my Dolls! Anna laughed. He does, doesn't he? But this baby is real and he is special and needs love. I am going to feed him now so be good, ok? Jerry and Anna nodded. They watched as Anna fed the baby and then changed his diaper.

Jerry replied mama is he going to stay that small? Anna replied no he is getting stronger every day. Peony was speechless and then said Anna you are a brave women to be able to care for this tiny boy with little chance of survival. Anna replied, we were told that he might only live a few days, but it has been a month, and he is still with us! Peony smiled and said that he is the cutest baby , you are so lucky to have such cute children. I only hope that God will bless Frank and I with children someday. Peony knew that the doctor's had told her she was barren.

Chapter # 2

Two months after Tom was born, he was still alive and making wonderful progress. Anna's mother and father returned from Ireland and were surprised to see baby Tom. Anna, I thought that I was going to make it home to see your new baby born. So, when did he arrive? Anna replied August 4th. Annie, Anna's mother replied oh, I thought that he was only a few days old. Mom, you have missed so much. Tom weighed only three pounds when he was born, and the midwife said he would maybe only survive a few days. I guessed he proved her wrong, because as you see he is two month's old! Johnny said that the baby was small but he is some what of a story teller. It was hard to believe this if I did not see it for myself.

If I had not seen it with my own eyes Annie said with a smile on her face. Anna's father Thomas replied you have beautiful children just as all the Rafferty's do. Anna said Pop we hope to have many more children as you and mom do. Tom began to squabble around the cradle that Anna now put him in. Anna still kept Tom in front of the large window where he slept for the last couple of months. The months passed and Tom kept getting bigger and bigger. Autumn to winter, winter to spring, spring to summer. Tom was growing and growing and growing. August 4th 1936.

The Rafferty and the Phillips families had a huge family reunion and birthday party for Tom. They all wanted to get together to celebrate the fact that this baby has survived his first year that so many had said that he would not see. The priest that blessed Tom one year earlier told

Anna that even though he had the faith in God to do his will he could not believe in the miracle in front of him. Johnny picked Tom up and said hi my little Tom Thumb! Jerry said Uncle why do you always call him that? Johnny laughed and said do you remember the story that I read to you called Tom Thumb? Jerry smiled and said my brother is not that small, not like a Thumb! Johnny just laughed and hugged Jerry and said I love you squirt! Jerry ran to play with the other children.

There were so many people at the picnic that day. Everyone ate like pigs. They were all stuffed with the good Irish food that Anna and her mother cooked. They ate Hamburgers, Chicken, Pot Roast, Red Potato Salad, Macaroni Salad, Cake and Ice Cream, Mince Meat Pie, and all the Irish Beer a person could drink and don't forget the coffee.

After dark Floyd had a special surprise for everyone. They ask everyone to go to the field across the street where the fire-works took place! Oh what a surprise! Many of the people began clapping and saying what a wonderful way to celebrate the end of the day. After all the fuss was over, Tom began to fuss. Anna excused herself and went to put Tom and the other children to bed.

The next morning Anna woke up feeling ill. She began her chores as usual, making Floyd his breakfast of bacon and eggs and coffee. Yum! That smells good Floyd replied. Just than Anna ran out the back door! When she returned Floyd said you don't look so good. What's the matter? I'm not sure but I think I could be pregnant again. I don't know if to be happy or sad. I guess if I am pregnant we should be happy since we agreed to have a big family. That only gives us more children to love. I'll call the doctor Anna replied. We need to find out as soon as possible so that we can try to save for the midwife again.

Anna took Jerry, Josephine, and Tom to her mother's house so that she could go to town to see the doctor. Annie asked Anna, How are you today? Anna said I feel sick and I don't know if I can handle having another child at this time. Annie replied, it is hard to be a mother, now I guess you know what I am going through! Mom It is hard enough for us feeding three children. God knows that Floyd is a good farmer and he said that he could work in town at the saloon calling some square dances on the week-ends for more money. Well Mom, I should get going, I'll be back as soon as I can.

As Anna arrived at the doctor's office she felt faint. Hi I'm Anna Phillips I have an appointment with the doctor. You don't look so good,

Lilly the doctor's nurse replied. Here eat these soda crackers and sip on this water this should help. Try to fill out this form the best that you can, the doctor will be with you soon. After a short while nurse Lilly called for Mrs. Phillips to go with her to an exam room. I know I must be pregnant Anna told Lilly. The doctor will be with you shortly, so just make yourself comfortable.

After a few minutes Dr. Fitzpatrick entered the exam room. With a smile on his face he said, "Hi there Anna so what's the trouble?" You don't look so well today. Anna replied with a low voice I'm ill. I guess I could be pregnant. How many months has it been since you missed your period? Anna replied about three months! "Well I believe that it is most certain that you are pregnant," Dr. Fitzpatrick replied.

Let's draw some blood and we will be certain in about three days or so. In the meantime I will go ahead and give you a pelvic exam. Anna just lay back and I'll check for the tell-tale signs. Well Anna I am 90% sure that you are with child again! Please try to take care of yourself in the meantime. I will call you in a few days with your test results. Thank you doctor. I'll wait for your call. See you Lilly. Probably on my next visit!

While Anna was in town she thought that it was a good idea to stop in and see her brother (Frank) and her sister-in-law (Peony). Anna walked the two blocks to their apartment trying to not get ill on the way. Anna soon arrived at the house and knocked on the door, to her surprise the priest answered the door! Anna said is my brother here? Father Francis said not at this time! Leona is here. She is in the kitchen! So Peony, where is Frank? He is working late today.

So what brings you here? I wanted to tell you both about me being possibly pregnant. Peony shouted Oh! What a wonderful thing! You know how Frank and I love children. Yes Anna replied. So how are you doing Father? I am doing well. I was just asking Peony about you and your family.

She has been a big help in the orphanage. She has also been helping me with some church events, raising some money for the kids in the orphanage. You know how much we love children, even though we have not been blessed with any as of yet. Well as you can see Anna said, I think I have my share right now with Jerry, Josephine, Tom and possibly one more. Father Francis spoke up and said well you know Anna God has a plan for you and he will take care of you and your family.

Peony said, "Anna I love children and you know that Frank and I will help in any way that we can." Well it has been nice seeing you both, Anna replied, I should be getting back since I did tell mom that I would be back as soon as I finished with Dr. Fitzpatrick. I'll call you in a few days when the doctor calls me about my test results. Tell Frank that I'm sorry I missed him see ya soon. Than Anna turned and walked away.

The entire drive back home all Anna could think about was how she would be able to care for and feed another mouth. Anna returned to her mother's house and said Mom I'm back! Well how did your appointment go? Annie asked. Well the doctor thinks that I am pregnant and that he will call me in a few days with the test results. Well, Annie replied you will have your days, and your hands full.

Josephine said to Anna Mama, "We missed you where have you been?" I have been down town to see the doctor baby girl, Anna exclaimed. Are you sick Mama? No I'm not sick Anna said. I went to see if we are going to get another brother or sister. Josephine's eyes lit up, I hope we have a sister that I can play with. Well maybe we will get you a sister, Anna said laughing. Sister, sister, sister Josephine sang as she ran down the hall.

Jerry said Josephine, what are you singing about? Josephine spoke up and said I am getting a sister! Oh Brother Jerry said, go play with your baby dolls! You dumb girl! Anna said, what are you two fighting about? Josephine said that she is getting a little sister, Jerry began saying. Well you see Jerry, Ma was at the doctor today and he thinks that we will be getting a baby. So where is the baby and when will it come Jerry said. Anna said enough about this until the doctor calls to let us know for sure. Ok Ma. Jerry said with a frown. Jerry go and get your brother Tom because we have to go home to make your pops dinner. Tell your grandma goodbye and give her a kiss. Oh Ma, Jerry said and then did what his mother ask him to do. See ya later mom Anna said as she hugged her mother goodbye.

Their house was just down the lane and it made it easy for them to get home just in time for Anna to cook for her family. Anna told the kids to color in their books while she made dinner. Just as she was mashing the potatoes Floyd walked in saying so what's that wonderful smell? Well what a way to greet me Anna said. We are having your favorite, Roast Beef, mashed potatoes and gravy. It sounds good Floyd said.

How did you make out at Dr. Fitzpatrick's office? Well he thinks I am pregnant again but we will know in a few days. So how was your day? Anna said. It was just fine. Where are the kids? They are in the front room coloring. Everyone was quiet during dinner as the day seemed like it would never end. Anna thought that it would be an eternity before the doctor would call back with the news good or bad.

The next few days all went the same at the Phillips residence when the telephone rang with Dr. Fitzpatrick on the other end of the line. Anna the doctor said. We have the results of your lab test. Anna gave out a sigh! Yes Mrs. Phillips you are with child. I thought so doctor. I have been sick every day since we last spoke. Anna, Dr. Fitzpatrick said you are due in March. I would like to see you in my office in one month. Ok Doctor, I'll see you then. Goodbye Mrs. Phillips. Than with that said they hung up the phone.

That evening Floyd came home from a hard day at work, he seemed very stressed. How was your day? Anna asked. It was ok Floyd began saying. So what's new with you? Any news from the doctor? Yes Anna said. We will be expecting our bundle of joy in March. Don't worry Floyd said. I am happy we will be fine.

Chapter # 3

March 9, 1937 a baby girl was born. Her name would be Eva Marie Phillips. Anna was happy to have another girl. As soon as Anna was feeling well Anna asked Floyd to go and pick up the children from her parents so that they could meet their new sister Eva. Hi Mama Jerry said as they entered the house. Hi all of you, I have missed you. So who wants to meet their new baby sister? Josephine said right away, me, me, me. Well all three of you come here and look how cute she is. All three children said oh she's cute with a giggle. Josephine said Mama when can I play with my little sister? Anna laughed; you will have to wait a little while before you can play with her. She has to grow a little. With that answer, Josephine said ok then. I guess I'll just have to wait.

Life for Anna and Floyd had been going by as usual until the summer of 1941. Anna was pregnant again. The depression was on and the Phillips family was living hand to mouth. Floyd was working two jobs and was trying all that he could to keep his family together. The news of another pregnancy was hard to hear. Anna was very ill with pregnancy it was very hot for mid-July. Anna's mother Annie came to the house every day. She would clean, cook and take care of Anna's four children. Annie vowed to help Anna with her house and children until the new baby would arrive. Annie worked tiredly for the next five months.

December 7, 1941 was a cold, cold day in Montrose, Pa. This was the bombing of Pearl Harbor and the labor and delivery of Anna's new daughter. (Pearl) named after the day! WWII, was at the beginning and a new baby was born to Anna and Floyd. As rough as life was for the Phillips family it only got tougher. The winter was hard and baby Pearl became sick and she passed away at only three months of age. Anna and Floyd were devastated. Anna cried so much, it put her in a deep depression. Once again Annie came to help Anna.

Knowing that Anna needed to have some time to heal, Annie called Frank to come and pick up the four children. So once again Jerry, Josephine, Tom, and Eva went to live with Frank and Peony. The next two years were hard on Anna and Floyd. The war was still raging when Anna gave birth once again this time she had another son who was named Carlton. Peony and Frank was still taking care of the other children and thought that it was about time for them to return home to their parents.

It had been two years since the death of Pearl. Upon the visit from Frank and Peony, they saw that Anna was still in a state of depression. Anna what can Frank and I do to help? The kids miss their mother and father! I guess I must try to move on with my life, Anna said. Let me try to take care of them for a while again. Anna you know that Frank and I are always here for you if you need our help. Thank you Peony and you too Frank for everything. We really love you both!

Summer seemed to come fast. Floyd was carving a large stone out in the shed. Anna went to the shed to give her husband a cold drink. Floyd! What are you doing with that large stone? I can't tell you right now. Go in the house Woman! It's a surprise! Anna said oh, I wonder what it could be? Don't worry you'll know soon enough. Anna just turned and walked away.

Anna decided to call Frank and Peony to come over for a picnic. Upon their arrival the kids ran out of the house shouting Aunt, Uncle. mama look who's coming, it's Peony and Frank. Floyd didn't have any idea that company was coming but he could hear the car coming and decided to leave the shed to see who was coming. Hey, what brings you here? Anna didn't tell ya? Tell me what? Floyd said. Before Frank could answer Anna said by the way, I invited them to dinner! Great Floyd said. I'm glad to see you both. I need to talk to you Frank, in the shed. Fine, what about? I'll tell you when we get there. Anna and Peony went to the house.

Look at this Frank. What a nice lamb. You did this Floyd? Yea. I carved the lamb on the top and I carved the inscription on the front of the stone. Our Little Angel.....Pearl Phillips Born Dec. 7, 1941-Died March 1942. Wow! What workmanship! Frank said in amazement. It is the nicest grave stone I have ever seen! Do you think Anna will like it? Floyd asked. I believe that she will think that this is the most special tribute to your daughter. I know that you both had a great loss and you will forever miss your girl Pearl.

Will you help me load the stone into my pickup? It will be my pleasure, Frank said with a smile. Floyd and Frank put the stone on the back of the truck and took it to the family cemetery. The two men put the stone on Pearl's grave. Once the stone was in place, Floyd said a prayer. Lord keep my child in your hands, an angel now in heaven she stays with you Jesus for you to care for and she to love in God we trust, Amen. With tears in the eyes of both men, Frank says to Floyd we must tell Anna to come and see this beautiful stone that you made with your two hands, and see it where it stands.

Floyd and Frank arrive to the house. So where did you two disappear to? Anna, do you remember this morning when I was working in the shed? Yes! Well I made something that I want to show you. What is it Floyd? I think I should show you, it is in the family cemetery. The cemetery, Why? I'll show you. Peony, Do you mind watching after the kids why we are at the cemetery? Sure, just go.

As Floyd and Anna arrived at the family plot, tears streamed out of the couples eyes. Anna looks at the stone I made for Pearl. You carved that lamb Anna said with emotion that only a grieving mother could understand. Floyd, what a wonderful way to show your love for our daughter. I can't believe that this is what you were doing all this time in the shed! Wiping away the tears, Floyd said to Anna I did this for us. We have now left an everlasting tribute for our little girl. Anna put her arms around Floyd and said I love you!! I love you my heart and everlasting love. We should get back to our children. I agree. I'm starved. I guess Frank and Peony think that we got lost or something. With that they both laughed and went back to the house.

So how did everything go at the cemetery? Peony it was hard but we have passed a milestone today. We should all eat. Frank has cooked the chicken, hot dogs and hamburgers. Thanks again for all you have done. While everyone was sitting at the table eating, Anna said I will always wonder about Pearl. What she would have been what she would look like all grown up and I will miss that. Anna, she is in God's hands now. He has a place for all of us. Just trust in him. I will pray for you all Peony said while patting Anna's hand.

Peony, I'm sure that Frank filled you in on the stone that Floyd carved for Pearl. Yes he did mention that Floyd has a wonderful talent for carving. Frank said that he engraved the front and carved the lamb on the top is that right? Yes he did Peony. It is the most beautiful thing I have ever seen. I know my baby sleeps with the angels. I felt the spirit of God while we were at the cemetery. I feel more peaceful than I have felt for quite a while. I know that losing your baby has left a huge hole in your heart. God does know and will help if you just ask.

I hope that you will continue to let me help with the kiddos. I will be glad to let you and Frank see them any time you want to. Why don't you help me get the little cherubs to bed? I would love that. Anna you know this is just what we all need, a night to just talk and unwind. Yea. We are going to play some cards when we get these little monsters to sleep. Oh, Anna you are too much. You know you are going to be ok. I know Peony, I know. The kids were all sleeping. Let's go girls, us guys are getting restless.

Keep your shirt on Floyd! We'll be right down. The table is all ready, let's say girls against the boys Frank said. Sure, be ready to lose your shirts Peony said as she and Anna were laughing. As midnight rolled around the ladies were winning. So you two double crossed us Floyd said. We should have known you two always beat the pants off us guys. We know that you have some kind of secret code. Anna and Peony laughed, secret code, secret code. So what do you say Anna? Should we call it a night? I guess. It is after my beauty rest time Peony said. We'll see ya, Floyd, and you too Anna. Bye Frank you sore loser. Anna gave a smile to Peony and they both hugged and said goodnight.

Chapter # 4

1945, life was still the same for Anna and Floyd. Floyd was still working in the farm and calling square dances. The only difference is that they now had another son by the name of Francis. The children were growing up rapidly. The eldest son Jerry was now 16, Josephine 13, Tom 10, Eva 8, and Carlton is now 2 years old. This new baby just arrived a couple of months ago. The Phillips family was pretty happy although their house was getting small. Times were hard. Anna was taking care of the kids and Floyd was busy trying to make enough money to feed his six children. At times Peony and Frank still stepped in to help with the children.

Tom especially had a fondness for his aunt and uncle. He seemed to love staying at Frank and Peony's house as much as possible. The children were either shuffled to either Frank and Peony, Matt and Grace (aunt and uncle) or Grandma Rafferty. WWII was very rough on so many families. Floyd spent many nights in a Tavern in the town of Montrose calling square dances as well as drinking.

One evening or early in the morning Floyd was driving home on an icy snowy road when all of a sudden there was a crash! Floyd flipped his car and the driver going the opposite direction also flipped his car. Floyd was able to get himself out of the mangled wreck. He ran for help. Floyd walked and crawled to a farm house that was miles away from the crash. Frozen and feeling ill after reaching the house Floyd collapsed. The gentleman of the house helped Floyd to the sofa and telephoned the local police. When the police arrived at the scene of the wreckage they found blood everywhere. Upon finding the other car driver the police noticed that he was not moving and he seemed to be dead!

The ambulance took the second driver to the hospital where they pronounced him dead on arrival. Anna was up worrying about Floyd when he didn't make it home as he usually did. As Anna waited in her chair drinking a cup of coffee, she saw flashing red lights coming up the drive way. Then a knock at the door. Mrs. Phillips open up, it's the police. Anna opened the door. Oh my God! Is he dead? Where is Floyd? Anna was crying hysterically now. Hold on Mrs. Phillips. My name is Officer Miller. Floyd has been in an accident, but he is not dead. He will be fine. He has cuts and bruises. He needs his rest tonight. He is a few miles away in a farm house, safe and warm. He will be home tomorrow. The other man was not so lucky. He was a DOA. Anna was shaking all over and crying uncontrollably. Shouting over and over again God help us please!!!!!! If you have any questions you can call us at the station, ask for Officer Miller. Try to get some rest. We will be back in a couple of days to talk to Floyd. Goodnight Mrs. Phillips. Thank you Officer. See you soon.

The sun came up very fast. Anna had been sobbing all night worrying about Floyd and wondering what happened. She tried to smile when the children woke up one at a time. She knew that her eyes were puffy from crying and was going to have a hard time telling the children about their fathers where-a-bouts. Tom was the first to wake. Where is Pa. Did he get up early? No your Pa was in an accident last night. Nothing too much to worry about he is going to be fine. Just go and play and try not to worry.

Noon came and Floyd was not home yet. Anna had a hard time putting on a smile and hoped to hear Floyd's voice soon. Soon after Anna had started making the kids lunch she heard that familiar voice calling Anna where are you. Floyd I'm in the kitchen. Floyd went to the kitchen, I'm home. I'm sorry I worried you. I thought you were dead last night when the cop came here. Anna began to cry. What happened Floyd? I killed someone he answered. I, I was driving home. I know I had too much to drink and the weather conditions were not as good as they could be. Oh I'm in pain. I don't know what to do. What did the police tell you? The police only said that you were hurt and they will be here in a couple of days to question you. I was afraid you would say that. I can't go to jail! I have too much to lose. My wife, children my dreams. Don't worry Floyd.

Maybe Officer Miller just has to complete his report and he just wants you to confirm the road conditions. Don't worry, don't worry you say I killed someone and you tell me not to worry. Who in the hell was in this accident anyway Anna not you. It was me me me!!!! Calm down Floyd. You need your rest. Go to our room and rest and I'll bring you some soup and coffee. Maybe it'll calm your nerves. As Floyd was changing his clothes memories of the crash kept playing over and over in his mind. He thought was it my fault? I know I had too much to drink. Was the road really icy? Could I have been able to stop, OH MY GOD I KILLED SOMEONE!!!! Floyd knew that at this point the life of the Phillips family was going to change forever.

As promised officer Miller did go back to the Phillips house to speak with Floyd. Floyd did give his statement about the accident and the events as he wanted the cops to hear them. In the end the report was filed that the weather was the fault of the accident and Floyd seemed to be out of trouble for now. Anna's father Thomas passed away in the spring of 1948. The rumors of the night of the accident were still going around town like wild fire.

The police returned to the Phillips house several times with more questions. They were trying to find out the "Real" truth about that terrible night. Floyd was getting scared and just wanted to get out of Montrose for good. Anna, Floyd said one night after dinner. I want us to move to New Jersey! What are you saying Floyd? I want us to start a new life. Look Anna I have a friend who has a farm there for me to go to work. We can buy that house we want. New Jersey has jobs. Let's try it out, please? We will be five hundred miles away Floyd! What about my mother? We can't leave her alone. We are all grieving over my Pop. What about the kids and their schooling? Anna we can work it out.

Let's go talk to your mother. She may join us when we get settled. Floyd, Annie said. You just missed the police. They were here asking questions about the kind of person you are and about you're drinking habit and stuff like that. What you told them, Floyd replied. I said that you keep to yourself. They know that you call square dances and they know that drinking is involved, so I didn't have to say much.

So what is on your mind Floyd? Well Ma, Anna and I have decided to move to New Jersey and start a new life. Would you like to join us when we get settled? Johnny said so where are you going? I believe Pennsgrove. You know the guy I work for in the tavern has a brother who has a farm. He said that he has a house for us and then when I make a little money I can send for the kids and you. I want to get a good job and buy that house that I have always wanted. Ma, I think that is the small town where your cousin Nora Siebert lives. You are right Johnny. It is in south Jersey. Hey maybe Jerry and I will go down and check it out for you Ma. I think that is a good idea. The kids can stay with me and Frank. They will be fine. I give you both my blessing. Good Luck!

We will be leaving on Friday, Ma I am going to miss you. Anna had tears forming in her eyes, but she knew that she was going to see her family again real soon. Friday came along real fast. Floyd and Anna stopped at Frank and Peony's house on their way out of town. Anna explained to the children that she and their Pa would be out of town for a while and that they would be back to get them when they got settled in New Jersey. She hugged each and every one of her children and said goodbye with a lump in her throat and a tear in her eye. She said I love you all. Take care until we meet again.

Chapter #5

The drive to New Jersey took about six hours. Floyd found the farm just outside of Pennsgrove without much trouble at all. Floyd pulled into the driveway near the small house and a man appeared. I see you found me Floyd I presume? Yes this is my wife Anna. I'm Bud Edwards. I'll just let you two get situated in your new home. Here are the keys. The house seemed cozy. It had a bedroom, kitchen, living room and was too small to bring anyone else to live there. This is small Anna moaned. I know honey, it will do for now. Just think we are starting our new lives as of today. We will be able to get better jobs and a bigger house in a couple of months. I hope so Anna sighed.

Floyd and Anna woke up to a knock at the door. Hi, too early? No. Anna was just saying that we need to get some food. We hope that you can tell us where the stores are. Better yet since it is Saturday, and I am not working today I will be glad to drive you two around and show you where the stores are in the town of Pennsgrove. That will be nice of you Mr. Edwards if it is no trouble Anna said. I think we are going to like New Jersey, Floyd. What makes you say that my dear? Oh, just a women's intuition. I really like that Mr. Edwards, and the house is not so bad either.

Soon a knock at the door again. Oh, hi Mr. Edwards. Please call me Bud. Ok Bud. How are you making out in your new home? We will be just fine. But you know it is only temporary. You know we only hope to stay a while and then we want to get a bigger house to bring our kids here to stay with us. Sure I hope you will find jobs real soon.

In the meantime Floyd is welcome to work on the farm to at least feed you both. Thank You Bud, Floyd smiled. So shall we go to town? I'm ready Anna said.

We need to fill the ice box with all kinds of food I'm hungry. Yea, and I haven't had my coffee yet and I'm a bear without my coffee. After driving about ten minutes Bud said oh, I didn't think to ask if you wanted to go to some other place except Pennsgrove. I think food is food and a store is a store Anna chuckled. Well here we are in downtown Pennsgrove. This looks like a nice place.

Many stores, it seems like a nice place to raise a family. I miss the kids already. "Me too," Floyd said. So how many children do you have Bud said. We have six we would have had seven but one died. Sorry for your loss. I guess you love kids, you have a bunch. Anna just laughed. Look Floyd a hardware store, drug store, laundry, bank, butcher oh so much. I like it here already. I think we should set up a home here. Look Anna a movie house, schools. We have already done our shopping. That was a nice butcher shop. I like buying fresh meat. Just think we could of gotten eggs on the farm. Why didn't I think of that this morning? I want some bacon and eggs when we get back and a nice big pot of coffee. Yea, I'm hungry. Let's go and see if Bud is ready to bring us back.

So did you kids find everything you need? Yes and more Anna said. I'm hungry let's get back Anna can make some breakfast. Ok Floyd, let's go. Upon returning to the house Bud helped bring in the groceries. Bud how would you like to bring your family for Sunday dinner? Sure Anna what time? What do you think Floyd, about four? Sure Anna four is good. Well I'll bring the misses and the kids tomorrow. See ya than.

What a beautiful day, umm what smells so good? I'm cooking you bacon, eggs and scrapple. The coffee smells good too. It must be the new coffee pot that we bought yesterday Anna added. I suppose you would like a cup? That would be a good idea, Anna. You think you're funny. Ha Ha. A new coffee pot and you want all the coffee to yourself Floyd mumbled to himself. Breakfast is about ready. I'll set the table. While eating breakfast, Anna was thinking to herself how it may be the right move to have come to New Jersey and how she could feel the black cloud that was over her family in Montrose was already lifting.

Out of the blue, Floyd stated I am so happy to be able to have this second chance with you my love. So what are you going to make for our dinner guest? I will be making my Roast Beef, Mashed Potatoes, Hot

Macaroni Salad and Green Beans. Dessert will be Minced Meat Pie. Yum, that sounds wonderful. Why don't I help you with the breakfast dishes? Anna laughed knowing how Floyd felt about doing house work. What is so funny Anna? Floyd, you are so funny sometime. You never do dishes or any other type of house work; you said that stuff is for girls! Honey, it is time for me to change. We are going to have many more happy years. I want us to have the American dream.

Four o'clock came fast! Bud should be here shortly Anna is dinner about ready. Yep! I have everything on warm. Just than a Knock at the door. Hi bud. Who do we have here? This is my wife Lena, my son Michael and daughter Molly. It is nice to meet you all Floyd said. Would you all like to sit at the table? Dinner is ready if you are all hungry now. Would you like some help in the kitchen? Sure Lena, I would like some company while I put the food on the serving plates. Anna started out by bringing out the Roast. Wow! That looks good Bud said. We are so blessed to have met you Floyd said. This is our way of saying thanks. The food sure is good Lena said with a smile. If you think that is good, you should try Anna's Mince Meat Pie it is out of this world.

Anna had a twinkle in her eye that has not been there for quite a long time. She was feeling so good about the new friends that were helping them make a new start and the possibility of reaching their dream. I want to thank you Bud for the opportunity that you are giving to us, you know starting our new lives and all Floyd said with a big smile. Anna nodded. We truly enjoyed the company and just to let you know it is nice having you both here on our property. I have enjoyed meeting my new friend, Lena smiled. Now I have someone here who I can exchange recipes with. They all laughed, well I hate to cut the day short, but we do have to get up early tomorrow morning. Six a.m. comes real fast Bud said. I'll see you than. Goodnight, Anna and Floyd said at the time.

The next morning Anna was already in the kitchen cooking breakfast and of course the coffee was on the stove. Good morning, breakfast already? Sure my man has to have his food before he works. I guess I do. I didn't expect you to be awake at five a.m. though! Well what good is it to send my husband to work with an empty stomach? I want to live our lives to the fullest; even if that means that I have to be up before the roosters! Floyd laughed. Well that was a good breakfast. I'll see you at lunch, around twelve.

For the couple of months, Anna and Floyd's routine was the same. Early to bed, early to rise. Until one day Anna went out and started looking for work. She came back with some news for Floyd. So how was your day? I'm tired as usual. What did you do all day? I got a job! A what? A job I said. Before you say anything just listen. It will help us get a bigger house and we can bring the kids here sooner. So where is this job anyway? It is at a factory called DuPonts! Well I have news for you also. As much as Bud likes the way I work he told me about a place that pays good money. Bud took me there this afternoon. It is the DOD. (Gun Powder Factory) Bud says that we can stay here as long as we need to and I can work for him on weekends. At this rate we will have a house in a couple of months.

Chapter #6

How was your day? It was unbelievable! Anna I have news for you. I took it upon myself to rent a house for us in Pennsgrove! Does that mean what I think it means? The kids can come? Anna, soon they can. We need to wait just a little longer. Floyd knew that he was lying to Anna but, he knew that it would only be a couple of days until his family would be back together. I guess I can wait a little longer to see the kids. I guess they won't be here before school starts in the next two weeks though will they. No Anna. We probably won't get to see them until the first of next year. Anna had a sad look on her face. Floyd was having a hard time holding in the surprise that it was not going to be next year but, next week.

Anna and Floyd went to the used furniture store to get some things for their new house. I like this lamp! It will look good in the front room. Look at this sofa and chair! This is nice stuff for being used. I think we should get the boys those bunk beds and the girls the metal framed beds from over there. Why? Those beds are so ugly! We can wait! As you said the kids aren't coming yet so we don't need those ugly things right now! While Anna was looking at a bed and a chest of drawers, Floyd was telling the man to deliver the beds to the back of the house while they were picking out the other furniture for the house.

Upon arriving at the house, Lena and Bud were waiting on the porch to help with the moving process. Hi, Lena how are you doing today? Great! Well let's go and look around our new house while the men help the furniture guys bring in the furniture. There is the living room, dining room, kitchen, pantry, upstairs look at the bedrooms, we have three. We even have a large attic. This is a lovely home that you and Floyd found. Well thank you Lena. It needs some work. Floyd says that he can paint and fix up the attic for extra room for a couple of the boys. How would you like some coffee Lena? That will be great. Come into the kitchen. Have a seat there. That chair was already here.

The men should bring in the furniture. What happened to them? Anna said wait here. I'll go and look outside. I didn't see them anywhere out front. Did you see them Lena? No! I was just sitting here watching the coffee cook. It seems to be done. I'll pour myself a cup. Yea! I want to see where those rascals went to! Anna went out to the back yard. Floyd! Where are you?

She could hear voices but couldn't see anyone. Soon Floyd came out of the shed. What's wrong Anna? I was just wondering what you two were up to. Not much. Just go inside. We will be bringing in the furniture as soon as the men bring it here. I thought they already did! Well they forgot some of it, so Bud and I will be talking in the garage until they come back. I hear some noise out front. Let's see what is going on. The furniture finally arrived after an hour of waiting. Let us men bring in the furniture while you ladies make us some sandwiches. We want to help Anna said. No! We can do it. Yea, Anna if the men want to do the lifting than just let them.

The next couple of hours Anna and Lena put away what they could from the boxes while the men arranged the furniture. I want to go to our room and put our clothes away in the closet and make our bed is it ready for us? Sure Anna. After that though Bud and I have one request. We really would like you two to go out to the house and pick up anything we forgot and make sure that the place is as clean as we found it. I think we could do that. Do you have any objections, Lena? No! I think the boys want to be alone. Lena played along with the plan knowing what Floyd was doing.

Floyd we're back! Where are you? Let's go up stairs Lena. Floyd! What are you doing? Where did those beds come from? We can't afford new beds! Wait Anna; do you remember those ugly beds? So what about them? Oh are you saying what I think you are saying? I sure am, I painted them all! We don't need those beds yet. The kids won't be here any time soon! Floyd began to laugh. Don't laugh at me Floyd George Phillips! Wait! Anna before you get yourself in a tizzy!

I have a surprise for you! Calm down! I have been lying to you. I have wonderful news for you. Sit down on the bed. I sent a letter to your mother and asked if she and Johnny would like to bring the kids to us. Anna began to cry. That is why you wanted those ugly, well now beautiful beds so soon! Yes and we will be needing to go tomorrow to get two more. Johnny did say something about maybe staying with Nora for a while.

The next week seemed to go slowly, even at work. Saturday, I wonder how long it'll be till the kids get here. I don't know exactly Anna, but all I know is that in the letter your mother sent to me it said Saturday one week before school starts. I'll wash the breakfast dishes Floyd and then we can relax on the porch while the weather is still good. Anna went out to the porch to join Floyd. Want a smoke? It might help to calm my nerves. I think I'll get another cup of coffee, would you like some? Sure, that'll be real nice.

Anna went into the house and fixed the coffee and put the cups on a tray to bring one of them to Floyd. As she neared the front door she could hear laughter. Floyd was trying to get the kids to be quiet but it was too late. Oh my God! You're here! The first kid she saw was Tom. I missed all of you. She hugged each and every one as they got to the porch. Come on in ma. I missed you. I missed you too Anna. Kids go on up stairs and see which room is for you. Look at your new beds!

Ma, I hope that you will not be hurt; I am going to stay at Cousin Nora's house with Uncle Johnny. You have enough people here and I need to look for a job. Maybe get married or something. Sis what a nice house, bigger than your other. Thanks Johnny. So how was your drive? It was not bad. The directions that Bud gave to us were very good. We called him last night. Oh he didn't tell us. Floyd we thought that we were trying to surprise you both even though you knew that we were coming.

Well Johnny I think that what you all did was lovely in spite of what I was going through. I'm sorry Anna. Floyd wanted us to surprise you. You weren't supposed to know anything about us coming here but, Floyd started feeling guilty about not telling you. They all laughed. Ma, Eva shouted I found my room. I have a pink bed. I love it. Josephine soon arrived in the room. What are you telling Ma Eva? I like my pink bed. Yea, I like my bed too. They look like twin beds. Both Pink! My favorite color Eva began laughing.

Ok you two go up and get your brothers it is time for dinner. Where is Ma, Johnny? I told her to lay down in your room. I hope that it was ok. Sure. She seemed tired from that long trip. She is worn out. You know it has been hard on her since Pa died. It has been hard on all of us. So many changes in such a short time. How has Floyd been these days? He has been a much better man to me lately. He even helps me out in the house. Is he still drinking? You know the answer to that one. He will never stop. Slow down, but never stop. I hope he doesn't get in trouble again. I can't handle much more.

Enough about me Johnny! So what are you going to do for work? I already talked to some men about a possible opening on the Rail Road. I told them that I had a lot of experience from working in Montrose. That is great Johnny. I hope you stay around. God knows Floyd needs someone to keep an eye on him!

Chapter # 7

The week went by quickly. Tom was getting ready for school. Wake up everybody it's the first day of school! Shut up, you act like you like school Josephine said. What did I hear you say Anna said. No one says shut up here. Get your lunches and eat your breakfast. I made oatmeal. Oatmeal, eeewww ! If you don't like it than go to school, Anna said to Josephine. Tom ate his already. He said it was good. He eats anything anyway Eva said. Look at the school it's so big! Eva don't be a baby! Don't worry Josephine; I'll bring her to her class. Just go on to your school.

Don't forget I am going to Re-Hi I'm in high school now. Don't be a show-off! Come on Eva. You'll like school. Eva felt scared most of the day until recess when she met a girl who started to talk to her. Hey I know you Eva said. You live on my street. Is your name Cindy? Yes! You came from some place far away, right? Well kind of. All the way six hours or something. Montrose, Pennsylvania. Tom also met many new people.

One boy always stuck out in his memory. All of the other kids called this boy racing stripes. Tom thought what an odd name for this boy, he seemed so nice. After school Tom ran to the kitchen to tell his Ma about the day. Mom, I have to tell you about the lice in our school. What about it? The lice jump from desk to desk and the kids all play with them with the tips of their pencils. Don't let me catch you playing with lice. I don't want to see any of those little critters in my house. Just keep your hands to yourself.

What else did you learn in that school? I met a boy, his name is racing stripes! What? Racing stripes! By now Tom was laughing so hard he was turning purple and was holding his sides. He has a problem with his nose! What? His nose, still laughing Ma he wipes his nose up and down his sleeve both arms, racing stripes!!! Anna couldn't help but laugh. Ok Tom enough be nice will ya? I don't laugh at him in school. He is nice and he is my friend. I hope you don't laugh it is not nice.

The school year passed by quickly. Tom was thinking about going to work for the summer. Even though Floyd was working Tom wanted to make his own money. He would be going to Re-Hi. Anna had to quit her job at Dupont's to take care of the babies.

Chapter # 8

The summer of 1949 the Korean War was in the start. Men 18 and up had to sign up for the draft. Jerry received a letter from President Harry Truman stating that he may be drafted. Jerry went to his local recruiting office and signed up for Army training. At dinner that evening everyone seemed to be quiet. Jerry had come to his parent's house to share some important news. Why is everyone so quiet? Jerry has some news he wants to share with all of us after dinner. What news? Floyd I just said he will tell all of us after dinner.

Everyone ate supper fast. Slow down! Are you going to a fire? Ah, Pa we just want to know the news. I'm sure it can wait Anna said. No Ma it can't wait. Let's all go to the living room. Ok Jerry if it is that important to you. It is important to all of us. Jerry began to speak. I have signed up to go into the Army. What? I don't want those bastards to draft me! They are sending letters to men like myself saying that they may get drafted. So I chose to go. I don't have a future here. I don't have a girl. I don't have nothing! I am going to get the hell out of New Jersey!!!

Tom immediately left the room. Jerry found him in the attic. What are you doing here squirt? I don't want you to fight. You won't come back here and those Korean's will kill you. I came up here to ask you if you wanted to spend the summer with me? Why? What's the point? I wanted to see my country before I went to fight in another country. I just thought that my favorite brother would want to go with me on this trip. I do want to go with you. I don't want you to die. Why are you going? I have to. You know they will draft me if I don't go. I know.

Ma, where is Pa? I need to ask both of you something. Let's go sit in the kitchen.

Pa, I was thinking that since after basic training I will be sent to Korea to fight. I would like to ask you if Tom could travel around the country with me for a couple of months. I think that would be alright. Is it ok with you Anna? I guess our boys are old enough to make their own decisions! When will you leave? In a couple of days. I hope you don't mind if I stay here until Tom and I go on our trip? That will fine. It will be like the old days when I would go to grandma's house and sleep in your room when you lived with her. I know that seems like a long time ago.

Tom and Jerry were talking in the bedroom about their plans for the trip. Where are we going first? Arizona, The Grande Canyon! Next New Mexico, California, you name it we're going. What are you boys up to? Josephine how did you get in here? I've been here all along. I heard everything! I was in the closet. I'm going to tell ma that you are going to run away from home with Jerry. You stupid girl, ma already knows what Jerry and I are going to do!

We should lock you in the closet for being so nosy! What about it Jerry for old time sake? What is all the racket about up there? Ma Jerry and Tom are running away. For your information your father and I already know about Jerry's plans. It is none of your business anyway. Now go to Bed!! Ha Ha I guess we told you so.

Jerry are you sure you want to do this? Yes ma. Well if you change your mind you know that you can stay with us until you go to Fort Dix. No, ma we want to go. I made you some sandwiches in case you needed them for the road. I thought you wouldn't change your mind. Tom hugged his mother. Jerry followed. I'll miss you boys. Jerry and Tom got in to the car, are you sure you want to do this with me Tom? Yes! Let's get moving. Step on it!! I need to get away from those people. Me too Tom. Me too! Let's go west young man! Jerry drove south toward Virginia. They went to North Carolina for a couple of days.

I like the Blue Grass Music down here. I like watching the girls square dancing. They dance with other guys, swing your partner round and round Tom began singing and laughing. They stayed at the roadside café and listened to all the country western bands until two in the morning. We need some shut eye. Where are we going to sleep? I saw a road side pull-off just about in the Cherokee Indian reservation. We can sleep in the car and in the morning we'll wash up in the restroom. I want to get to Florida and take in some sunshine. We can stay there for as long as we want to. I think it will be fun. I'm tired. Let's get some sleep so we can get to a good start in the morning.

Welcome to Florida. What? Welcome to Florida that is what the sign said back a couple miles. Are you sure Tom? Yep. Look at the palm trees! It is so beautiful here. Let's find some beaches. I want an orange, I'm hungry. Jerry drove a couple hundred miles to Miami. Look! Blue water, I love it here. We're going to stay here a few days. We'll go swimming and get in some fishing. We can camp out on the beach. Are you sure we can do that, Jerry? Yea! It'll be fun just wait and see. Tom, how did you like Florida? I really liked it. I hope Texas is as nice as you say it is. It will be Tom. We are almost there.

I hope so, it seems like we have been riding in this car for days. It has been, we are almost in Texas. Just a couple more hours. Look at that! At what? At that armadillo. A what? Tom ask. An armadillo!! I was wondering what that was. They're good eatin' Jerry said laughing. I hope you're kidding, because I know they're not for me. Just kidding Tom. We're going to stop in Dallas. I just saw a sign that said Dallas is just ten miles.

Texas was a little sandy, don't you think? Well it is a lot of desert out there. What did you think it was? Jerry said. I think I like Arizona much better, Tom said. I like the chaps you bought for me in Texas. Thanks, any time. Would you like to stop to eat? Sure Jerry. I am a little hungry. The Grande Canyon Restaurant, What a name! Tom, it is appropriate due to where we are. Isn't that Canyon beautiful? It is amazing.

We learned all about it in school a couple years ago. It is bigger than the history books describe. Jerry can I call home while you get us a table? Sure, don't be long though. Hello operator! Can I please be connected to a New Jersey operator? Sure, I'll connect you. Number please? AXY-4851, this is a collect call operator. Thank you I'll connect you. Hello, Will you take a collect call from Tom? I sure will. Hello Ma! Tom is that you? How are you two doing? We are great! I was just calling to check in and let you know that we are ok! That's good son, tell Jerry I said take good care of you. He is ma, I have to go. Jerry got us a table, were about to eat supper. Alright Tom, call me again soon and take care. Goodbye ma. Goodbye Anna said with a choked up voice I love you!

Whistling, Jerry said to Tom look at the legs on her! Hi, fellows. What will it be? Two burgers, Fries and Cokes. Coming right up, boys. What brings you fine young men to these parts? I'm going into the Army. Well damn! I'd like to get to know you better. Sorry honey, we are going to California tomorrow. Yea Tom said. We are traveling before my big brother here goes off to fight the war. Well your supper is up. Let me bring it to ya with a piece of fresh cherry pie on the house. Well thank you Miss. It's been a pleasure the waitress said. No the pleasure was all mine, Jerry smiled.

California, I don't know what the fuss is all about! Tom, it's about movie stars, fancy cars, money, girls. And what pretty girls they have out here too! Tom said. I like the blonde hair and blue eyed babes. Jerry that is all you have on your mind. Girls, Girls, Girls. It doesn't hurt to look. I'm going away anyhow so I miles well enjoy the scenery. Jerry, I hate this state. It is always raining. That is what happens in Washington. I didn't know we were coming to Washington. I wasn't, but I thought we might head back east. Maybe go to Maine or Massachusetts, perhaps Vermont? We can't leave here until this storm stops. We are low on food, Jerry.

Well we can't go anywhere there is zero visibility. All we have to eat are the Banana's and water we brought with us from California. I know, Tom. I'm sick of eating those Bananas's too. I can't wait till this storm ends. It rained for two days straight. Tom and Jerry were stuck at a road-side pull off for two days straight. They ate the Banana's and slept in the car. Jerry in the front seat and Tom in the back. Good morning, good morning yourself. Where are we? Vermont. What is here? The scenery Jerry said. We are stopping here until tomorrow. I thought we'd go up to the mountains. Those guys over there told me that there is snow up there. We could get a cabin for the night. That sounds fun Jerry. Do you think we might get to fish a little? Yep Tom there is a pond near the cabin. Good. I want fish for supper. It sounds better than those Banana's any day, Jerry laughed.

Welcome to Massachusetts! When will we be in Boston? In less than a few minutes. See there is the Charles river. We are going to camp out down there for a couple of days until we get to New York. Look! There is Paul Reveres house. This is so cool! I have had a history lesson around the country. Tom, just wait until we get to New York. You will love it. I

Love Boston. One day I am going to live here. Sure you will Tom Jerry said with sarcasm.

The next morning Jerry and Tom woke up to music. It was in Spanish. I wish I can understand this music, Tom said. Me too Jerry said. Get my guitar out of the trunk. I want to play with the band. Hi, amigo's. Hello! Can I play with you? Sure! Jerry just joined right in playing a few tunes and than he said Thank You. We have to get on to New York. It was evening when Jerry drove on to Amsterdam Ave. Look at the bright lights Jerry. I Love New York. That is the slogan, Jerry said.

Soon the two reached Time Square. This is the city that never sleeps, so we won't sleep. Let's go have some fun. That night Jerry took Tom to every Bar that was open. Jerry didn't have much money left and he didn't drink too much. Look at the Statue of Liberty she is bigger than I thought she was. Tom do you remember Grandma ever talking about Lady Liberty? Yes. Well that is her, and over there is Ellis Island. That is where Grandma and Grandpa came into the country at. They had to register their names and where in Ireland they were from.

Where are they from any way? Ireland I told you! Jerry I mean what part of Ireland. Tippery, Ireland. It is in the southern part of the country. Oh, I guess we will be going back to New Jersey soon. Tomorrow. I wish this trip would never end, Jerry. I don't want you to go away. I don't want to go either. I really don't see that I have much of a choice. You know it is that I am damned if I do and damned if I don't!!

Chapter # 9

That sign said Montrose. I thought you said we were going home, Jerry! I know I didn't say what home. I thought it would be nice to see our relatives up home before I go away. Let's stop by Aunt Margaret's house before we go to the old house. Ok, Tom? Do you think she will be home? It is late afternoon. She should be home from her job at Dr. Ramsey's. I'll knock to see if she answers the door. Not if I beat you to the door first Tom.

Hi, boy's! When did you get here? Just a few minutes ago? Where is Jerry? He will be here. I'm here, Jerry said out of breath. Come on in boys! Go wash up! I'll see if I can find something for you two to eat. I hope not Corned Beef and Cabbage! We had plenty of that when we used to stay here. Tom chuckled. I hope she didn't hear you say that. She does have big ears. We are all washed up, aunt Margaret. Good, I hope you like BLT's? I'm making Corned Beef and Cabbage for dinner. I know it's your favorite, Tom. Yea Aunt Margaret, I love it.

Tom was kicking Jerry under the table who was trying to hold back the laughter. So, how is Uncle Frank and Aunt Peony? They are doing well, Jerry. I hope they will have time to see us. Jerry said that we will be only staying for a few days. Where are you boys staying? At the house. Jerry, that place looks like a jungle. The grass is as tall as I am. Well I guess I'll have to cut it. I'll help too Tom said. Would you boys do a favor for me? Sure Aunt Margaret. What can we do for you? Tom, Could you go to the store down the street and get me some Cabbage? That's Ok Aunt Margaret. You don't really have to cook for Tom and

Me. Don't be silly boys I love cooking for you. Ok Aunt Margaret. We'll be right back.

Aunt Peony! How are you? I'm doing well. Uncle Frank will be glad you two are in town. Your Cousin Frank will be glad to see you too. What are you doing here? "Buying some Cabbage for Aunt Margaret." "Cabbage? Yea" Tom said. It seems that is all Margaret knows how to cook! It sure does Aunt Peony. Well we'd better be going. We have to get this Cabbage back to aunt Margaret. Well we will see you boys. Goodbye Tom and Jerry said in unison.

Sorry Aunt Margaret. We ran into Aunt Peony in the grocery store. Seems to me you got lost Jerry. Aunt Margaret I'll finish sweeping the side walk for ya, Jerry said. And I'll help, Tom said. Dinner is at four o'clock on the dot! Don't be late. We won't, Jerry said. Don't even think about running off either. We'll be right here. Ok boys let me go get dinner started. I'd like to run off Tom said while laughing. That Corned Beef was the best you've ever made. Why thank you Jerry! It sure did hit the spot. Thank you Aunt Margaret.

We really have to get down to the house before dark. You know that there is no electric out there? Yes Jerry, I have a flashlight if you need it. It will be fine Aunt Margaret. Tom said that there is a couple of Kerosene lamps in the kitchen. Well I hope you boys will come back to see me before you go back to New Jersey. We will Aunt Margaret Tom and Jerry said in unison. I really did like Aunt Margaret's Corned Beef, Tom said. So did I. It is a real shame that everyone makes fun of Aunt Margaret and her Corned Beef. I sure have missed everyone here. So have I.

Being out there on the opened road has made me realize how much family means to me. So why go to that stupid war anyway Jerry? I just have to, Tom. Why? I don't want you to go. As Jerry's car neared the house you could see the tall grass and of course the wild flowers. This place has been rejected very badly. It is going to take us a full day just to cut the grass Jerry said laughing. By the looks of things it may take our few days that we are going to be here. Not if I can help it Tom. I want to visit some old friends, and old places that I used to hang out in. I'm glad we made it here before dark. This place has not changed. Tom, do you have your lighter with you? I sure do.

I'll go ahead and light the lamps. Open some windows! This place smells. It is just a musty smell from being closed up for so long, Jerry said. It smells like old socks to me. Have you been smelling old socks lately, Tom? No!! I, never mind. Look, Jerry! I found those Pictures that Ma asked us to bring home. Good, I have a list that Ma gave to me on the Phone the last time that I spoke to her. What is it Jerry. Just some pots and pans, pictures, blankets, etc. Do you want to sleep in your old room, Tom? I don't think so. Why not. It is too hot here. Tom, I think you are right. It is probably a good idea that we sleep in the living room anyway.

Jerry, I miss my bed in New Jersey. I have enjoyed our trip, but I really am ready to go home. Jerry you're up early. I couldn't sleep on that hard floor. You could have slept on the couch, or in my bed. I guess I could have. Guess what I found? What Jerry? Coffee. Oh it is probably old. Not the way Ma stored it. It was under the cabinet. It is always so cool down there. You know the way Ma always stores her mayonnaise and ketchup. That's right they never go bad. I thought Ma had her coffee pot in New Jersey. No, Tom she forgot it here. Ma and Pa bought a new one when they went shopping in New Jersey.

How do you like your eggs, Tom? Just barely cooked. You mean over light? I guess that's what you call them. Jerry, I got the old lawn mower out. Thanks, we should try to get the grass looking good. At least cut down some. Don't forget Ma and Pa will be coming here next month for the Rafferty reunion. I didn't know that they were going considering the circumstances on why they left here. Jerry, Ma told me that Pa will be kinda laying low. Ooh! Let's get the chores done so that we can go and have some fun tomorrow. What do ya think we will do tomorrow, Jerry? Go see Uncle Frank and Aunt Peony, maybe go down to Grandpas farm and ride the old tractor; You'll see Tom it'll be just like old times.

Tom, do you have the hamburgers ready? Yep! I sure do. Good the grill that Pa built is already for cooking on. Look who is coming! It's Frank and Peony. Frank waived and had a huge smile on his face. I'm glad to see you boys. We're glad to see you again too Uncle Frank, Jerry said. I brought my famous Potato Salad. Um. I miss your cooking Aunt Peony Tom said. I'll set the table. We are eating at the Picnic table aren't we? Yes aunt Peony. Unless you would like to eat inside. I know how you hate the bugs! I do Jerry, but it is a nice day and I want to remember this day forever. You act like you will never see me again!

Jerry, your mom told me that you will be going to the Army soon and that you will leave for Korea after Boot Camp. Is that right? That is right! I will be leaving on the second week of September. Do you mind if I say a prayer for you Jerry. I guess it won't hurt. Ok, well let's hold hands. Dear Lord, we first ask you to keep your hand upon Jerry as he goes to Korea. Keep Jerry safe from harm Dear Lord. Keep the spirits up for all the troops fighting this war? Also bless this food. In your name we pray. Amen.

After a few minutes of silence Jerry said so how are the Burgers and Dogs? No complaints here Frank Jr. said. They are great Peony said. Everything is good Frank said. I am enjoying myself with you boys again. This is just like old times. Would you boys like to play some cards with us? Yep, Uncle Frank. Is there some Cards here Frank ask. I think so Tom said. Look in the Buffet right behind you Aunt Peony. Look under the Tablecloth's for the cards. Why, Tom. Because Ma would hide the cards there so that us kids couldn't play with them. Well let's get started Frank Jr. said. Can we play rummy? Sure Jerry said. The five of them played rummy for about four hours.

Well I think we should go, Frank said. Yea we have been messing around a lot today. What are you guys going to do tomorrow? Frank, Jr. asks? Maybe we'll go swimming. Do you want to come with us, Jerry said? You bet! I have some things I want to ask you guys? Sure, we will pick you up around nine or ten, Ok? Yea see ya than said Frank Jr. Tom and Jerry woke up sweating. Good day for swimming don't you think? I guess it will be! Are we going to pick up Frank Jr ? I will Tom. I told him around nine or ten. It is already eight thirty. I am ready to go if you are Tom. I wonder what Frank wants to talk to us about? I don't know Tom. We will soon find out. Jerry, I was wondering if you were coming for me. I told you I'd be here and here I am. I was worrying!

Frank Jr. it is only nine thirty. I know I want to get there before Charlotte gets there. She will be there? Sure, Tom! She always asks for you too! For what? She always talks about the time that you almost drowned. Oh brother! That's all I need! Tom just be cool, like I taught ya. Listen to your big brother Jerry for once will ya? Upon arriving at the Lake Frank Jr said, so am I adopted? Yes you are. You came to live with Aunt Peony and Uncle Frank when you were five years old. Do you remember? Not exactly. I always thought that she was my Mom.

She always took care of me at the orphanage. I don't know where I come from, who my parents are nothing.

I can't help you there, Jerry said. Me either, Tom also said. Hi Charlotte! Hi Tom! Long time no see. Where have you been? I've been in New Jersey! I live there now. Why New Jersey? I don't know. Well It is good to see you again Charlotte said. I must be going, my girl friends are waiting for me. Goodbye, Tom! Goodbye, Charlotte! Ha Ha! So Love still blooms! Don't be an Ass Hole Jerry! Frank and Jerry just laughed. The boys swam for most of the day. We should get you home Frank Jr. Thank you guys for taking me with you. I'm going to miss you both. We are going to miss you too Frank. Tell your Mom and Dad goodbye for us! We are going home in the morning. I think I want to leave real early. I'll see you Frank Tom added.

Chapter # 10

Jerry, I would like to thank you for all you have shown me this summer. Thank you Tom for going with me. You will never know how much this trip has met to me. I mean the time we spent together. I have made a decision, Jerry. What decision? I am not going back to school. I know all I need to know right now. I am not going to High School! What is Ma and Pa going to say about this, Tom? I don't know! Probably good riddens! I was thinking about going to work for Mr. Carpenter. They will like the fact that I will bring home money. I will learn how to paint, put up siding, shingle roofs and so on. It will be a good learning experience in itself. Tom was daydreaming about working with Mr. Carpenter. So, here we are? The cemetery? Why the cemetery, Tom said. I was supposed to bring some flowers for Pearl's and Grandpa's graves.

I saw a little greenhouse a couple miles back. Thanks Tom! Let's go and get them so we can get on the road. That's it right ahead! Look at that there is a lot to choose from. I'm not sure what we should get. What do you think, Tom? I like the Peony's. Well Peony's it is. May I help you gentleman? Kate, how the hell are you? So, is the rumor true? Are you going to Cucamonga? It sure is except it is Korea, Jerry said. Well it is Cucamonga to me!

So what the Hell are you two doing in Montrose? We have been traveling. Tom and I are going home today. I did hear that you were traveling. Something about California! What's that all about? Well Tom and I thought that it was a good idea for me to see my own country before I go to fight for another country! We have been on the road for most of three months Tom finally said. We went to, too many places to tell, but we surly enjoyed ourselves!! We sure did Jerry said. So what brings you to this greenhouse? We need these Peony's for the cemetery. Oh! I'm glad you stopped by here, Kate said. I hope to see you boys again real soon. Good luck cousin out there in Korea. She hugged Jerry than Tom. I'll miss you. I love you both.

Kate walked away with tears flowing down her cheeks. She thought she would surely never see her cousin Jerry alive again. That was strange to see Kate don't ya think? It was so nice to see her Tom. I didn't know that I was going to feel this emotional when I decided to sign up for the Army! Back at the cemetery Tom and Jerry stood by the fence. The water is so peaceful here. Those Peony's look good on the graves. It was a good idea coming here. I know Ma will be happy to find out that you put flowers on the graves. Tom, we must be going. It is already noon!

I wanted to leave this morning. I will be glad to get home to my lumpy old bed back in New Jersey, Tom said. Me too! Let's hit the road! Goodbye Montrose, hello New Jersey! Jerry I'm hungry. Tom you are always hungry. Lucky for you I brought the rest of the hot dogs with us. There is a rest area about twenty miles from here. I hope so Tom added. I am so hungry. I must have a tapeworm! I think you do. They both laughed. Well here we are. We can feed your tapeworm now.

Tom, we've been here for two hours now. We should be going. We are only about three hours from New Jersey. As the miles went by Jerry or Tom didn't say much to each other. Tom, what's wrong? You haven't spoken since we left the rest area. I know. I was just thinking about all we did together and the fun we had. I am sure glad we have had this time together. So am I little brother. I am going to miss you Jerry. I don't know if I will see you again when you go to Korea. I don't know either Tom. I will miss you too. So don't go. I have to go I already signed up for the Army. Better me going of my own will than being drafted.

I guess you are right, but I'm still going to miss you. I am going to miss you too. Look Tom! We are only fifty miles from New Jersey. Did you tell Ma that we are coming home today? No Tom I thought that we could surprise her. Ahh, we are home. Look Jerry, Ma is on the porch. Don't let her see us. I'm going to park up the street. Jerry parked the car than the two boys got out of the car and walked the block to the house. Anna saw Tom first. Where's Jerry? Anna said. He's right behind me. I'm here he said waving his hand. Where is your car? Ma I parked down the street so that you wouldn't see us. We wanted to surprise you. I sure am surprised! I thought you were not coming back until next week. That's what I told you Jerry laughed.

We thought that it was about time for us to come home and tell you all about our trip. I can't believe this. My boys are actually home. I have missed you both. Let's go in and let everybody know that you are home. Ma, let me move the car down here closer to the house. I did bring some of the things that you wanted from Montrose. I am going to get supper started. Don't fool around too much. We all want to know the details about your trip.

Can I go with you while you get your car? Sure Tom. We have all those boxes to bring in from the car. Well let's get the stuff so that we can take a nap before supper. I'm with you on that one Tom. I need a nap after our long trip. My lumpy mattress will feel good after sleeping everywhere including that old car. Tom just laughed at his brother. The Supper table was so noisy. Everyone wanted to ask questions all at once. Ok Floyd said. Enough racket. Jerry wants to talk first. Just to let you all know, Tom and I had the best time of our lives.

He explained in graphic detail about their journey including the desert and all of the wonderful people that they met along their way. We saw cactus, cowboys, all sorts of animals and we even ate snakes in Arizona Tom Added. I have brought back some gifts for all of you. Tom and I will pass them out after we finish with supper. Everyone took a place in the family room.

Tom you go first. Thanks Jerry. I have been talking about this all day. Carlton, this is for you. What is this? Open the box. Tom said. Carlton's eyes lit up as he pulled out a pair of chaps. Wow! Just like the cowboys wear. Are they for me? You know it Jerry said with a smile. These are just like the cowboys wear. Can I try them on? Go ahead Carlton. Let us see when you get them on Tom said laughing. Francis, you also have some in the other box. Wow! I got some too. I'm going to look just like a cowboy too.

And for you girls Jerry said, "We got you Indian dolls." Ma we got you a pair of moccasins and for Pa we got a snuff box to put your tobacco in. We picked up the chaps in Texas. All the rest of the stuff we got from New Mexico. Jerry and I also got presents. I bought a guitar and Tom got chaps just like the boys. Look Jerry, Carlton and Francis said. They are a perfect fit.

Chapter # 11

1950, Jerry was sent to Korea. The war was raging out of control. The radio was on at the Phillips house 24 hours a day. Floyd quit his job at the DOD. He found a job making more money as a mechanic in a garage in Mullica Hill. Ma, Tom said can I talk to you and Pa tonight? Sure I'll talk to him after Supper. What do you want to talk about? I was thinking about going to work for Mr. Carpenter. He says that he will teach me painting, plumbing and heating. He does travel quite a bit so I would travel to other states. Is this going to be a problem ma? I will tell your Pa tonight.

That evening, Tom decided to tell his father himself. Pa I have to talk about something with you. If it's about you going on the road with Mr. Carpenter, I already know. I think it would be good for you to learn how it is to be a man. You do know that Ma and I are looking at a house in Harrisonville. With the money that I make working for Phil Gardner we can afford this place. I hope that you buy this house Pop. It has been your dream ever since you came here. I think it will be good for us all. When will you be leaving, Tom? Mr. Carpenter wants me to leave with him in the morning. Then you should get packing than.

As morning came, Tom took his duffle bag to the porch to wait for Mr. Carpenter. Eat some breakfast before you go Anna said. I ate already. Just then there was a beep. Well I have to go. There is Mr. Carpenter now. Tom smiled as he took his bag of clothes and got into Mr. Carpenters truck. He waved goodbye until he couldn't see his Mother's face any longer. After traveling from state to state Mr.

Carpenter took Tom to Louisiana. This is great! We are in the middle of Bourbon Street. I can't believe you brought me to Mardi Gras! Well you deserve it Tom. You are my best worker. We will be going home in a couple of days and I wanted to do something special for you. I am glad you did Mr. Carpenter.

I've always wanted to see Louisiana during Mardi Gras. Tom, it has been a pleasure working with you. I will be calling you when I need some more help. Right now I am going to spend time with my family. See you soon. See you, Tom said. Ma, I'm home. What is with all the boxes? Oh it's you. I'm Glad you're home.

Tom you are just in time! In time for what? What's going on? We bought the house in Harrisonville. So where is the house? On Main Street. Pa will be glad you are home. I hope so. Oh he will be. He has been trying to get someone to help him make up the Garage into a small house for your Uncle Johnny to live in. Well, Ma I do have a lot of experience in building, painting, plumbing and so much more. That's good Tom. So when are we moving? As soon as the weekend. Pop will be glad to have the help. It would have been even better if Jerry were here.

Chapter #12

As the Phillips family settled in their new house in Harrisonville, bad news came from Korea. A telegram that read as follows: Missing in action, sorry to inform you that at this time your son Gerald is hereby not accounted for. No further information is available at this time. Sincerely, the US Army. Anna was devastated believing the worst. My son Anna Cried. What am I going to do. I know he is dead! Anna cried for a few days than to her dismay a knock at the door.

Anna opened the door to see a uniformed man, oh my god! It is true my son is dead! Ma'am. Please sit down, the gentlemen's voice was deep. I'm sorry to inform you that the Army has not gotten back to you sooner on the telegram that the Army sent to you. Anna began to cry. No, Mrs. Phillips what I am trying to say is that I am sorry for the misunderstanding. Your son is alive. He is in a hospital in Japan. He has been shot. He took seven bullets to his back. We thought he was missing since Pork Chop Hill. He was not. He lost his Dog Tags when he was trying to get out of the line of fire.

I guess by what we were told he was actually still alive when the next battle took place. So, how did Jerry get hurt? He rescued fellow soldiers from a burning tank near the Chosin River in North Korea on November 18th. Anna was crying uncontrollably. When will my son come home? He should be in the states sometime in the beginning of the 1951. This does all depend on his progress. You do understand he is not out of the woods as of yet? Yes I do. The Army will keep you informed of Gerald's progress. Thank you all for letting us know about my son. Mrs. Phillips we really should get going we do have so much to do. Thanks again. My prayers are with you all. Thank you Mrs. Phillips. We will be talking to you soon.

Two and a half months after the news about Jerry the phone rang. Anna was always terrified to answer. Hello, yes, yes, where? Thank you for letting us know. Goodbye. Anna than hung up the telephone. Is everything alright Ma, Tom said. Who was that? It was the Army. It seems that your brother will be flown from Japan to the Veterans Hospital in Phoenixville, Pa. We will be able to visit him by the end of the week. Pop will I be able to go with you and Ma to the Hospital? I'm sure you can.

Josephine will stay here with the younger kids. That very Sunday, Tom, Anna and Floyd went to the hospital. Anna said I'm scared to see Jerry. We don't know what to really expect. We will go to talk to the doctor when we get inside of the hospital. Anna it will be alright to let Tom go to see his brother first. I can Tom said in a voice of excitement. As Tom walked into Jerry's room he felt much emotion all through his body. He smiled at Jerry. Jerry said Tom, good to see you brother. Tom said no it's good to see you. I've missed you. Tom was holding back the tears.

I have so much to tell you. Pa has been building so much in the house. I guess they told you about Harrisonville? Jerry nodded. Pop built a house out of a garage, and you won't believe this, remember how we all played with marbles? Jerry nodded. Well Pop took them away from us and get this he put them in the porch that he built. Yes you heard me right. He said that we didn't know how to share them and he made a porch. Pop said if you can't learn how to share those marbles than no one will ever have them. Jerry tried to laugh. It was evident that Jerry was in much pain.

Anna and Floyd entered the room just as Tom finished the story about the marbles. Jerry, Anna said, I've missed you and I love you. Jerry had many machines hooked up to him. He could not talk too much the pain was unbearable. The doctors did tell Anna and Floyd that Jerry had a long road ahead of him. He said that Jerry would have to learn to walk again and that he would be lucky if he even does walk. The bullets were lodged near his spine and that one was still in his body and could not be removed in fear he would be paralyzed for the rest of his life.

No one really talked much that day. Everyone was very overwhelmed. Each week the Phillips family went to the Veterans Hospital. Jerry was getting stronger by the week. Physically Jerry was improving, but mentally no one knew the pain that he was feeling inside. Jerry would cry to himself about the men who lost their lives. The pain of knowing that some of his friends did not survive and the pain of knowing that he was called disabled from the war in Korea.

It had been an entire year that Jerry spent in the hospital. Floyd went one more time to the hospital. This time Jerry was coming home. As Floyd drove home not many words were said. When Floyd and Jerry arrived in Harrisonville, many of their family members and friends were there to celebrate Jerry's homecoming.

Jerry tried to enjoy himself but deep down inside he was hiding the pain and the memories that were too unspeakable to talk about. Jerry was in so much mental pain, he began to go out to bars and stay out all hours of the night. Tom was also spending a lot of time with his friends.

Chapter #13

1952, Anna was decorating the house for Christmas. Ma the house looks very pretty. Ok Tom what do you want? I was just wondering if it would be alright to invite a friend to Christmas dinner. Is it a girl? Yes it is Tom said. Tom, where did you meet this girl? I met her at the five and ten in Pennsgrove. My friend Bones introduced me to her. Does this girl have a name? Her Name is Shirley. I guess that would be alright. This will only be one more mouth to feed. Thanks Ma Tom said, while walking up to his bed room.

Jerry was sitting on the other bed playing his guitar. So I heard you ask Ma if you could bring home a girl for Christmas dinner. Yea, I did. So, tell me about this mysterious girl? Jerry had a smirk on his face. Is she pretty? Tom said with a huge smile, yes she is, and you can keep your paws off her Tom said joking. So give me some details! Well Jerry, her name is Shirley and she lives in Pennsgrove and goes to Re-High. She has a job at the five and ten and you probably want to know her age? She is sixteen. She sounds nice Tom. When will we get to meet her? I have a date with her tonight. I was thinking about bringing her to the house tonight. Did you tell Ma that? No I just thought I'd surprise everyone. So don't tell anyone. I won't Tom.

A couple hours later Tom arrived with his friend Bones and Shirley was behind. Hi, Bones. Hi Mrs. Phillips Bones said. Ma, aren't you going to say hello to Shirley? I'm sorry I didn't see you there. How are you honey? I am fine Mrs. Phillips. It is good to meet you. Ma, can Shirley and Bones and me talk to Jerry in the kitchen in private? Sure,

I'll keep the kids out. Jerry, I'm glad that you are in the kitchen. Hi, Bones, and this gorgeous woman must be Shirley? This is she. Tom you said that she was pretty, but you didn't tell me that she was drop dead gorgeous!

Jerry added, maybe one day I'll meet a beautiful lady to settle down with. What about Bea Beasley? She is my friend's wife, Jerry replied. She is pretty and single, Tom said. I know, remember she is my best friend's widow? I'm sorry Jerry. I just want you to be happy. You made your friend a promise before you both went to Korea. I know I did tell him that I would help to care for his family if he didn't make it. Jerry frowned. I do like Bea and I guess it would be alright if I did ask her out for some dinner. That's right Jerry. It is time for you to start living.

Tom you are so wise for your years! Jerry, I am friends with Mildred. She is Bea's sister. I could talk to her first if you would like me too. Thanks, Shirley. I just wonder what other people would say about me dating my best friend's wife. I really want to settle down and have a family. But, I'm not sure about a ready-made-family! Tom smiled at his brother. I think you should think about it. I know that Bea likes you. What do you have to lose? Jerry, believe me Mildred told me that Bea does like you very much. Thanks Shirley, you are so nice.

If it would make you feel more comfortable, we could go out on a double date. Shirley, that is not a bad idea. Jerry smiled for the first time in a very long time. Tom, where are you going tonight? Bones and I are going to pick Shirley up at her house and I don't know what we're doing other than riding around in Bone's car. Well I got to go, I hear Bones down stairs now. Bones yelled, Tom let's go! I have an eleven o'clock curfew! Jerry said, have fun and don't do anything that I wouldn't do!

As Tom and Bones arrived at Shirley's house they saw her waiting outside. Hey there Tom said; want to go riding around for awhile? I'll have to ask my Dad. Dad can I go out with my friends? Who are your friends Dute? Dad, this is Bones and his friend Tom. This is my father Leon or Mr. Norton to you. Hi Sir, Tom put out his hand and shook Mr. Norton's hand. Just be careful and have her home by ten. Yes Sir, Tom said.

We should be going don't ya think? Tom began laughing. What's so funny Tom? Your name. Dute! What the hell is a Dute? Shirley rolled her eyes. That is my Dad's pet name for me. Is there something wrong with my name? Shirley said sarcastically. No Dute, Tom said trying to control his laughter. I think it's cute. I think I'm going to call you Dute from now on.

Tom, Bones and Shirley rode around and ended up in Camden. Tom bought Soda's and a Sub and the three went to the Camden waterfront to eat and talk for a while. Ten o'clock came fast. Well I'm glad you got me back on time. My Dad would not let you take me out again if we were late. Well goodnight Shirley. Tom placed a light kiss on Shirley's lips. I'll see you on Christmas. Goodnight Tom.

Christmas at the Phillips house was always a joyous occasion. Anna made a huge Dinner and she took regular socks to make a stocking for each and every person who would come to her home at Christmas. The stockings always had nuts, fruit and candy. Tom brought Shirley to his parent's house for Christmas of 1952. It is good to see you again Anna said. I'm glad to be here with your family, Mr. and Mrs. Phillips. I have a gift for you Shirley, Anna said. She handed Shirley a stocking. Oh I love it! I have never had a stocking for Christmas. I'm glad you like it. Thank you Mrs. Phillips for being so thoughtful.

After dinner Shirley helped to clear the table. I'll help you with the dishes, Shirley said. That's not necessary honey. The girls will do the dishes. You just go and have some fun with Tom. I know you don't get to spend too much time together. He works quite a bit and you work and go to school. I don't mind helping out Mrs. Phillips. I would have to do it at home. Well that is alright you just go and have some fun.

Thanks, Mrs. Phillips. Shirley left the kitchen and sat on the sofa thinking to herself. Wow what a wonderful family. They really like me. If I were home I would have to do all the work. Tom soon joined her on the couch. So, Dute what would you like to do tonight? I just want to stay here and look at the tree and watch your family have fun. You really like my family? Yes I do.

Chapter # 14

1953 Tom was seeing a lot of Shirley and was hardly ever home. Josephine got married and moved out of the house. She had a small wedding. Floyd and Anna didn't like the man Josephine married so she didn't visit very much. Jerry and Tom were talking in their bedroom one night. They were having their usual conversation about the women in their lives.

So how's Shirley? She is fine. The same as usual. She is still fighting with her mother about babysitting her brother's and sister's. As I told you before Shirley's dad works all the time and her mother is always going out with her so called men friends. So I have not seen her as much as I want to. At least we have not had much privacy. I usually have to see her at the house since her mother always makes her baby sit. So how are you going to move your relationship to the next level if you don't have privacy? I don't know, Jerry.

One thing I do know, I am falling in love with Shirley. So how are things with you and Bea? I've been out with her a few times and I really think that she might be the woman for me, who knows? Jerry and Tom laughed. After a few minutes of laughter Jerry said I guess were just two wild and crazy guys! Anna called up to Tom. Come and get the phone. Who is it Ma? It sounds like Shirley, She is crying. Hello, what she did what? I'll be right there. Is it alright to bring Jerry with me? Yes Tom, come fast. I will see you soon Dute. Ok Shirley said, Goodbye. Goodbye Tom said and then hung up the phone.

Tom returned upstairs. Jerry would you go to Shirley's house with me? Sure, what's going on? Could I explain on the way to Pennsgrove? It must be serious if you are in a hurry to go. It is Jerry. Ok so now that we are in the car explain to me what is going on. Ok Jerry, let's just get on our way. You remember what I told you about Shirley's mom always going out with her so called men friends. Shirley had a fight with her Mom about babysitting. We had a date tonight and Mrs. Norton knew it. Shirley told her mother that she was sick and tired of cooking, stewed tomatoes or potatoes while her mother was out with men eating steak an fucking!

Shirley's mother hit her so hard that she flew across the room. Jerry said I think you should get her out of there and bring her home with us at least for the night. But what about Ma and Pa? What will they say if I bring Shirley home? Tom you have to tell them the truth about what has been going on in Shirley's house. I hope we get to Shirley before her Mother gets home. You mean to tell me she still went out with whoever when all of this took place? I guess so, Tom said. I'm glad you are here. Do you want to go to our house with us? Tom, all I want to do is to get the hell out of here. Let me get a few things. I'll see if Johnny can watch the kids for the rest of the night or until Dad or Mom comes home. Ok, Dute we'll be waiting.

Shirley came back to the car with a brown paper bag. Ok guys I'm ready! My brother Johnny is watching the kids for now. What are your parents going to say when you show up with me? Don't worry Shirley. Tom and I'll explain to Ma and Pa what happened and that you need a place to stay for a couple of days. So where will I sleep? In my room Tom said trying to not laugh. Shirley smacked Tom, you are a bad boy! Your Mom won't let us sleep in the same room. We'll just see about that! My family really likes you Dute! Ma will help you Shirley.

Since I am the oldest I will talk to Ma and Pa when we get to the house. After entering the house Jerry said Ma I would like to tell you both about a situation that is of a serious nature. But first Shirley and Tom are going to the living room to talk. So what is going on Jerry, Anna said. Jerry proceeded to tell his parents about the abuse that Shirley was getting at her house and that he thought it was a good idea for her to stay with them at their house. I thought that you were going to tell me that Shirley was Pregnant Anna smiled. We will be glad to help her.

Good morning Mrs. Phillips. Good morning Shirley. Did you sleep well? Have a seat here at the table so we can talk. I slept as well as I could. Mrs. Phillips I am having a rough time at home with my mother. Yes I know honey. Jerry explained what happened to you last night. I am going to talk to Floyd and ask him if we might be able to help you.

Shirley's eyes widened, what in the world can you tell my parents that I have not told them already? My plan will work just let me talk to Floyd. What plan? You've got to tell me! Alright! I was wondering what you think about living with us? Are you sure that is what you want, another kid? Honey you are the love of my son's life. Jerry has told us all about what has been going on at your house. We just want what is good for you. Of course this means you will stay with us and finish school. You can share a room with Eva. Thank you Mrs. Phillips. Don't cry Shirley. We really do love you.

Chapter # 15

January 1954, Anna and Shirley were in the kitchen when Anna said to Shirley, my son says he loves you? I guess he does, Shirley smiled. Shirley I know that you are not always sleeping in Eva's bedroom. Don't worry Honey; I know you love my son. It is Floyd. He thinks that you two should get married if you want to continue to live here. Are you saying that I can't stay here anymore? No Shirley that is not it. Tom has asked for your hand in marriage. Shirley smiled. You know the people in small towns. They are talking. Floyd said that he saw someone at the pool hall who was whispering about you living with us. I am just suggesting that you and Tom sit down and figure out what you want to do about this situation.

Hey you two, what is going on here? Nothing Tom. No, I know you better than that Dute. You and ma got quiet when I came into the kitchen. Why don't you just spill it? Alright Tom, Pa and I think that you and Shirley should get married. What! I thought that we were supposed to wait until Shirley got out of High School. Shirley has been talking about a June wedding. People are talking about you having a girl living with you here and we think its best that you get married as soon as possible.

Shirley will you be my wife? Yes I will. I'm sorry we can't have a June wedding liked you wanted. It will be alright Tom. I love you. So when will we go and ask my parents if we can get married? I'm sure they won't like me getting married but, I won't take no for an answer. I will be a good wife to you and I want to be with you for the rest of my life. Now everyone was being quiet. What's going on?

Shirley and I have been in the kitchen today. I taught her how to cook Pork Roast. She may need to learn how to cook for our son someday. Tom kicked Anna under the table. So as I said what is going on? You are up to something. Pa I have something that I want to ask of you and Ma. What is it money. Sorry son I don't have any to loan. No Pa, it's not like that. I would like to get married. Shirley and I have been talking about next month. Ma has been talking to you. Yes Pa that is what we have wanted anyway. The town's people talking just speeded things up a little.

So you kids want to get married? Yep! I love Shirley. We will go to see the minister tomorrow. I hope he can perform our wedding by next month. Do you want Pa and Me to help you two ask Shirley's parents about the wedding? Ma I am a man and I want to handle this on my own. I think we should go to see my parents as soon as possible. You know how news gets around. I am scared Tom. I hope that my Mom will sign the marriage certificate.

Jerry wants to go with us to your parent's house. That will be good. They might act more civil if we have someone to back us up. I will call home first to make sure that Mom and Dad will be home tonight. Ok, but don't tell them that Jerry and I are going with you. I bet that they think that Dute wants to go home, Jerry. I bet you a wooden nickel that is what is on the Norton's mind! Shh!

Hi Mom, could I come to see you and Dad tonight? Ok, I'll be there in about an hour. See you than bye. So, what did she say? She thinks that you want to come home, right? She probably thinks that I want something like that. I didn't let on. I just told her I wanted to talk to them. You two need to stop worrying about winning a wooden nickel Shirley said laughing. You both know way too much about my family! We should be on time Tom so I suggest you change your clothes and comb your hair. You could try to make a good impression. I guess I should change my clothes also Jerry said, even though I don't know why.

That is not going to be my future family in-law. They all laughed. Not too much was said on the trip to the Norton house. Ok Tom be calm and both of you be on your best behavior. Let me do the talking

Dute. Tom do you know what you are going to say? Don't worry; Jerry is here for moral support.

Hi Mom. So what are you doing here? Tom will explain. He wants to talk to you and Daddy. Let's all go to the front room and sit down. Pete, Tom and his brother Jerry are here to talk to you. I have a few things to talk to you about. Sure Tom what is on your mind? Just to let you know my real name is Leon. You can call me Mr. Norton. Sir this is my brother Jerry, Yes I remember you. So what's this all about? I am here to tell you that I love your daughter and that I intend to ask for her hand in marriage. So when do you think you will get married?

We thought that February would be a nice month. We know that we don't have much money and are not asking for a big wedding. We just want our parents at the ceremony. You can get married, but I don't want any part of this fiasco! I will sign the marriage certificate because that baby will need a father! Mom! I'm not pregnant! I just don't know why you and daddy don't believe me. You will both see in nine months if there is a baby or not! Shirley began crying. We just want to get married, we are in love. Shirley, Tom and Jerry got up and slammed the door as they left the house.

Shirley cried the entire twenty or so miles back to Harrisonville. Why won't they believe me, Shirley cried. It is because of our ages. I love you Dute that is all that matters. So how'd it go with your parents? Dute's parents said that they think she is pregnant and they don't want to go to the wedding. Norma and Leon will sign the papers. They said that we are too young to know what we want, but she was seventeen when she had Dute. You will show them Tom. As your big brother I can vouch for the fact that you respect Shirley in every way you can respect a wonderful women.

I want to be her husband. I am truly in love with her. you will be a good husband son. Just be patient and all of this mess will work out some how Anna said. We will be going to the minister tomorrow to work out the details. As the day approached for the wedding Shirley was exited for the wedding and of course Tom was excited for the wedding night. Shirley bought a blue ankle -length dress with matching hat and gloves. Tom bought a new blue double breasted suit.

Ruby, Shirley's best friend was her maid of honor and Tom's best friend Bones Sawyer was his best man. Their vows were short and to the point. At the end of ceremony the minister blessed the marriage. May your love last a life time, and may you have many blessings along the way. I would like to announce to you that from this day forward you will be known as Mr. and Mrs. Floyd Matthew Phillips Jr. Norma did show up to the wedding as did Anna and Floyd.

Tom and Shirley invited Ruby and Bones out to dinner. When they all returned from dinner Anna had invited some family to have cake to celebrate. Beer over flowed and everyone had a good time. When it came to bed time Shirley went to get into bed and there was the sound of crunch, crunch, come to find out Jerry had put crackers in their bed.

According to Shirley there was no love making on her wedding night due to the fact that Tom was too drunk to do anything. When Tom got into bed Shirley said one side of the bed broke. Tom was too drunk to fix the bed. A couple months later Shirley and Tom had a wedding reception. Shirley made her own cake and Anna cooked most of the food.

Chapter # 16

Several months passed since the wedding, Shirley woke up one morning in early November feeling nauseas and had thought that she may be getting the flu. After a couple of weeks of feeling this way she thought that she should ask Anna about seeing the doctor. Honey, are you feeling sick again? Mom yes I do feel very nauseas. Has it ever occurred that you could be pregnant? You do seem to have the symptoms of pregnancy. How long has it been since your last period? Mom, how embarrassing! I really have not thought about that.

We do use rubbers. Rubbers break Shirley. I guess my last period was in August. I know for sure that I didn't have one in September or October. My guess Shirley is you are about three months along. I guess I should call the doctor for an appointment. Have you said anything to Tom? Mom I really did not think about any of this. I thought that I was just going through some body changes. You sure are now Shirley!

You know that my Johnny is four and needs a playmate. As for my son Tom he will love a baby. He loves you and he will love his child. I just don't want to burden you and Dad. Look Shirley I know that times are hard. You two want to move out on your own and it is just not the right time. We will make room for a baby. A few days later Anna took Shirley to the doctor's office.

Just as they thought Shirley turned out to be three months pregnant. Mom, could you please not tell anyone about my condition? I want to surprise Tom tonight at dinner, and yes what a surprise it will be. Shirley and Anna were laughing. Shirley has some news that she wants to share with the family. Thanks Mom. Tom, this news is especially for you. Tom, you are going to be a father sometime in June. How can you be sure? TOM you know how a women gets PREGNANT!!! You think you are funny. Dute, you have just made me the happiest man alive.

Ok, Tom now we can eat. You know I am eating for two. December was always an exciting time in the Phillips house. Anna was decorating for Christmas. Mom look at me I'm fat! You are not fat Shirley. You only have a little bump in your tummy. Just you wait until you are seven or eight months along than you will think that you are fat. The kids will call you fat, fat the water rat. The two shared a laugh. I really don't know how you had so many kids. Shirley, I don't know either. Floyd just couldn't keep his hands off of me!

June 13th 1955. Shirley was having some pains in her stomach. She thought that they were gas pains. A couple of hours passed without the pain letting up. Tom, I think that I might be in labor. Let's go and ask Ma and see what she thinks. She has been through this so many times that she could even tell if you will be having the baby tonight. Ma, I think that Dute is in labor! Shirley why do you think that? I have been having pains similar to gas pains. Is it a constant pain? No Mom it comes and goes. I think that we should time the pain the next time that you get a contraction. Anna looked at the clock that was sitting in the bay window. Moms start timing. I am having sharper pain right now. Ten minutes later the pains kept on coming.

Everything is under control Shirley. I can deliver your baby right here. No Mom I want to go to the hospital. I don't want to have the baby here in the house. What's wrong with that? I had all my babies in the house. I need the hospital right now! Let's get going Tom. I really don't want to have this baby in the car or the house. Tom was so nervous. He was speeding all the way to the hospital. Tom slow down! I don't want you to have the baby in the car. I know what happened to your Mom when she had the baby in the car that died. I just want us to have a happy healthy baby not born in a house or a car. I want our baby to be born in a safe clean hospital.

As Tom stopped the car at the emergency room door, Shirley was in terrible pain. Dute, I will be right back. I will get you a wheelchair. Shirley felt better once she was in the emergency room being examined by a doctor. Mrs. Phillips your baby is on the way. I am going to send you to the maternity ward to get ready for delivery. Mr. Phillips you may go to the father's waiting room. A few hours passed, when a Nurse went into the father's waiting room. Mr. Phillips the nurse began speaking. Yes I'm Mr. Phillips. Sir I was sent to let you know that your wife and new daughter are doing fine.

When can I see my wife? As soon as Mrs. Phillips is cleaned up and we take her and the baby to the room we will come and get you. Tom has a huge smile on his face. He was going through so many emotions. Tom was very excited and was very nervous knowing that his daughter was now a reality. Tom smoked an entire pack of Winston Cigarettes between the time he was waiting for his daughter to be born and the time he then was waiting to see his wife and daughter. Mr. Phillips, you may go to see your wife as soon as you would like to. Tom didn't take much time to go to Shirley's side.

Tom is that you Shirley said as Tom walked into the room. Yes, it's me. Tom reached up and opened the curtain. Dute are you alright? Yes, but I'm real tired. Just look at her, She is so cute. She looks just like you Dute. So what shall we name you, Tom said to his Daughter. Perhaps after your Mommy! I don't think so! So what name do you want for her? I was thinking about Cheryl Norma Ann Phillips doesn't that sound pretty. Cheryl is short for Shirley, Norma for my Mother, and Ann for your Mother! I like it Tom said. She does look like a Cheryl. I thought that you might go for that name. Considering that it is like having three of the ladies in your life all rolled into one. They both laughed as the baby was sleeping in her little crib.

Dute, I really have to get going. I have to get up early for work. I'll come to see you again tomorrow night after work. Tom kissed Shirley goodbye. Even though Shirley was thinking yea sleep… he is probably going to the bar to celebrate. In fact that is what I know he is doing. Shirley thought to herself, I'm here suffering from the pain from having a baby. What the hell. I really don't care. I need to get some rest. I am a mother now.

As the next few days went by, Shirley learned how to bathe, diaper and take general care of her new daughter. Shirley was sitting on the bed when Tom entered the hospital room. Good morning Dute. How are my two ladies doing today? Are you ready to go home? We are doing as well as we can, and yes we are ready to go home. On the way back to the Phillips' house in Harrisonville Shirley was thinking about how nice it would be if the three of them were going to their own home.

That house is already too crowded, Shirley thought. I am going to come up with a plan that we get our own house. We need a house fast. December came by fast. Anna was getting ready for Christmas. As always Anna decorated her house to the nines. Tom was wondering how he was going to buy Christmas presents for his family. Tom had been saving money for an apartment. After all the little money he did make went to food and baby supplies.

Just as Tom was about to tell Shirley that he could not afford to buy the presents that they wanted to get for everyone, a big snow storm hit New Jersey. Tom was happy when it snowed. Carl, how would you like to make some money? Look at all the snow! We can make some money shoveling snow for people. Alright Tom.

So Tom and Carlton went and made enough money to buy presents and they even had enough left over to buy all of the trimmings for the biggest Christmas dinner you could imagine. Anna invited all of the family that could fit. Jerry and Bea came to dinner with her daughter little Bea and their newest baby Beverly. Yes, Jerry and Bea did get married in September of 1954.

Chapter #17

Shirley, you have had a bug in your ass all day. What is wrong with you? I know whenever you call me Shirley you are not happy. Tom, I want to get my own house. I want a place we can call our own. We need more space. Dute, you already know that I still don't have the money for a house. I'll get a job than. I don't care if you want to live with your mother all of your life, but I don't. Cheryl and I will get our own house. I don't give a fuck what you do. I'll leave your ass here and I won't let the door hit me in the ass on my way out either.

Tom and Shirley fought for quite a while that night but the next morning they were still not speaking. The next few days Tom and Shirley did not say too much to one another. Tom finally broke down, he said ok Dute, I can't go on like this. We do need to start looking for our own place. We can start looking this weekend. That weekend Tom and Shirley did go looking for a house. What they found was a two bedroom Apartment. And yes, it was big enough for the three of them.

They signed a contract to pay $25.00 a month! In 1956 this was a one week paycheck for Tom. Dute, don't say a word to Ma. I want to break the news to her myself. She will not want us to move to Pennsgrove. She will try to talk us out of it. Yea, She won't miss us, She'll miss the money we won't be giving to her anymore. Dute, I don't want to fight with you. I know that Ma does expect the money.

That is why I want to break the news to her myself. Sure Shirley thought, she will indeed miss the money and me being a built in babysitter and housekeeper! Tom and Shirley arrived back in Harrisonville feeling happy about their decision on renting the apartment. Hi, Ma. There is something that I want to tell you. I'll go get a bottle for Cheryl. Dute I'll be out in the kitchen in a while. Sure Tom take your time.

Ma, Shirley and I are moving out. Anna looked surprised! Shirley and I rented an apartment. I hope you will understand, we need the room and our privacy. I guess I knew that this day would come. I hope this means you want to have a few more kiddos. I know that we want more kids. But first all we want to do is to get settled in our new home. Anna gave Tom and Shirley some used furniture. It took some getting used to having an apartment all to their selves.

After a couple of months Shirley thought about getting a job to help out with some of the expenses. So what have my ladies been up to all day? You mean other than cooking and cleaning? Cheryl has been crying all day! You know, the diaper rash, teething, tiredness, and the normal baby stuff.

Ya know Tom I think I need a job! I could help pay the bills. I need my sanity. I could work somewhere part time. I could get a sitter. Wait a minute Dute! I am not going to let any wife of mine work. Who wears the goddamned pants around here anyway? Tom was so angry that Shirley would suggest such a thing. Shirley was furious that Tom treated her as if she was not worthy of working and taking care of a family. She didn't speak to him for a week!

Dute, we need to talk about this. Talk about what? Shirley showed that she was angry. I am a man. I was brought up to believe that a good man takes care of his family. I really do love you! You and Cheryl are my world! I want you to be able to enjoy our baby and keep our house clean. I love it when I come home and dinner is on the table. I make enough money to pay the bills and if times get tough I'll get another job.

You know God always does provide for us. I Love you both and I don't want to lose you. I love you too Tom. I just wanted to help so that we would have everything we need. Dute, we have each other that's all we really need. Tom and Shirley had come to an agreement.

Until one day in 1957 when Shirley had realized that she missed her period. Shirley decided that she wasn't going to alarm Tom about her findings until she went to the clinic. The next few days were hell while Shirley waited for the test results. Tom do you remember that night when the rubber broke? Tom looked like what the hell women, just spill the beans. I am pregnant again! Dute that is great news! I told you that we are going to have a big family.

Tom you think it's a picnic taking care of you and Cheryl. I told you that we are only having two kids. Dute you are so full of shit. We are going to have at the least three kids. You don't know what you're talking about Mr. We will be finished making babies after this one. We'll see about that Tom thought to himself. When is the baby due? The Doctor said according to him, early October.

If you want my input I can't wait until then. You men think that it's a Picnic being fat and pregnant. The months did pass quickly. Shirley cleaned her house all day on October 5th. You are really ambitious Dute. I bet that Baby is coming. What the Hell are you talking about? You did the same thing when Cheryl was born.

During the night Shirley started in labor. Tom! Get the Hell up. It is time! Time for what? Time to play! Shirley was not in the mood for Tom's sarcasm. Let's go. The baby is coming. Mr. Phillips, Your wife and new baby are fine. Is it a boy? No Mr. Phillips you have been blessed with a beautiful baby girl. Thank you Nurse. Tom thought to himself I guess I'll win. We will have three children after all. We need a Son. A boy to carry on the Phillips name. Dute, I saw the baby, she is so cute! I think we should name her Lucille. I'll name her shit first!

Tom, where in the hell did you come up with that name? I don't know, I just thought that it was cute. I already have a name picked out. I think that Terri Lynne Phillips has a good ring to it! Shirley smiled. Dute I really don't care what her name is. Terri is a pretty name for a pretty girl. Shirley thought to herself yea I knew that you would see it my way. A few days later Tom took his wife and daughter home from the hospital.

Mommy you're home! Where did you get that baby? Can I play with her? Be careful Cheryl, she's not a baby doll! This is a real baby. She is your sister Terri. My Baby Sister? That's right and she will be sleeping in your room.

Chapter # 18

1960 Shirley was pregnant again. Dute what have you been doing all day? The usual, why? The house looks great, are we expecting company? Not that I know of. One thing that I do know, my feet are swollen up like balloons and I'm tired. I need a break. It is hard work trying to take care of the house and two kids. That's funny; you wanted to get a job just a couple of years ago.

Tom, just shut the hell up. Dute I do have an idea, let's ask Gumby to move in with us. Are you sure that you want my brother living with us? You did say that he was having problems at home with your Mom. He said that he would help out with the girls and house. Are you sure that you want my brother living here? Dute, it will be good for you. I wouldn't have brought it up if I thought for a minute that it wasn't a good idea.

Thank you for being my husband. My pleasure Mrs. Phillips. Now who's king around here Tom said laughing. Gumby moved into the house in the next couple of days. Just as he promised he did help out even more than Shirley thought that he would. Dutie, it's been two month's now since I've moved in so I thought that I would cook a nice dinner for you and Tom. Let's just say it is an early anniversary present. I don't think that I could eat.

I think I'm in labor. I've been in pain most of the day. What's this I hear Tom said? Do you want to go to the hospital? No, I think it's just pressure, too early too tell. Dute, you said that you've been in labor all day. We are going to the hospital to get you checked out. Shirley knew that the labor was different this time around.

The doctor at the hospital said Mrs. Phillips so as I heard you have been in labor now for eighteen hours. After I examine you I am going to send you for an X-Ray. I need to find out if your baby could be hung up anywhere. Are you trying to say I need a cesarean section? I'm not sure Mrs. Phillips that is why I need to perform these tests. Doctor, I feel the baby's head Shirley said after returning from the X-Ray. It looks like we should prep you. According to the test results your baby will arrive soon. You will be able to have your baby the normal way. I hope so doctor, after twenty six hours of labor let's get the show on the road.

Mrs. Phillips, he's a big one. Did you say he doctor? Yes it's a boy. As the Nurse got Shirley situated in her room Tom came in with the biggest smile on his face. Ha, we finally did it! I guess we did Tom! We are now all done having babies. Dute, we've only just begun. That's what you think Floyd, and we are not going to name him Floyd either. I really hate that name. Do you think it's been a great name for me? Tom began laughing. How about Thomas? After my grandfather Rafferty. I like Thomas.

We need a middle name. How about Thomas Wayne Phillips? Dute that sounds really good. My Grandfather would have been proud. Dute, I should be going. I'll be up tomorrow to see you. I love you. I love you too Tom. Shirley drifted off to sleep. Tom, I've been waiting for you all day. Where in the hell have you been? Dute, I have a surprise for you. What now? Just wait until we get outside, I'll tell you all about it. Shirley got in the wheelchair and the nurse told Tom to bring the car to the front of the hospital.

Where is he Shirley thought to herself? Than a brand new Mercury, Comet parked right in front of her. Shirley began thinking to herself, what a jerk! Don't they know that I am waiting here with a baby to be picked up? They'd better move fast or Tom will be really mad. Just than the man got out of the car. To Shirley's surprise it was Tom. So Dute how do you like our new car? I guess this is what you needed the checkbook for. I thought that it was a good anniversary present and a thank you for finally giving me my son.

1963: Shirley was pregnant once again. Tom what are we going to do with another baby? Who is to blame for this pregnancy? What are you saying Dute? It is obvious. If I tried those birth control pills I might not be pregnant for the fourth time. Well Dute, I couldn't be happier. Tom that's what you always say. You are not the one who has to carry around a baby for nine months. Dute, I hope we have ten more. I don't think so mister, I'm going on the Pill after this one is born.

It might teach you a lesson if I keep my legs closed. Don't be silly Dute! I know you love being knocked up all barefoot and pregnant! Why don't you try it if you think it's funny? I wish men could get pregnant. See how you would like to go through the pain and labor. As this pregnancy progressed Shirley had become tired and had gained much weight. Her legs and feet were swollen.

Dute, how are you feeling Tom said as he sat down at the kitchen table to drink his morning coffee? I'm hot and tired. We need an air conditioner. I can't take the heat any longer. I'll see what I can do tonight. Maybe I can get us one. I know one thing Dute. You need your rest. Doctor Atlig said that I should put my feet up and try to stay in a cool place. Could you bring me some strawberries? I have been craving them for days. That evening Tom did come with the air conditioner and the strawberries. Shirley did eat many strawberries during her pregnancy.

June 1st Shirley cleaned the house feeling as ambitious as she usually did before she would go into labor. As early morning approached Shirley said Tom, it's time. Wake up Gumby; we need to get to the hospital now! When did your pain start? About 12:30 or so, why? Dute you have plenty of time. I don't think so, my water already broke, and my pain is only a few minutes apart.

The hospital was only around five minute from the house but to Shirley it seemed like an eternity. Tom parked the car in front of the emergency entrance of the hospital. Tom grabbed the wheelchair that was sitting inside of the emergency room doors. My wife is in labor Tom said to the nurse. Tom helped Shirley into the wheelchair and wheeled her directly into the emergency room.

Mrs. Phillips how far apart are the pains the nurse asked? Around three or four minutes. Well we should bring you up to the maternity ward ASAP! I am going to have Dr. Atlig exam you Mrs. Phillips. Hello doctor. Mrs. Phillips you are going to be awhile. I am going take a nap. The nurse will call me when you are fully dilated. As the doctor and the nurse left the room Shirley screamed, doctor come back I can feel the baby's head. The baby is coming.

Mrs. Phillips the nurse said you do know that you will be awhile. No, the baby is coming look I feel the head! Doctor Atlig come back here Mrs. Phillips is going to have this baby right now. Ok, Mrs. Phillips let's get the show on the road. I guess I am not going to take a nap right now. In the next few minutes Shirley delivered an eight pound girl at 2:38 a.m. Mrs. Phillips is it ok for me to get a nap now or is there going to be more surprises?

They all began to laugh. Tom, I guess we are girl making machine. Dute, what do you want to name her? I was thinking about Linda. I have always liked that name. So Dute, since we now have four kids I think that we should make it five since you wanted two and I wanted three. I don't think so Shirley said in a disgusted voice.

October 1963, Tom, I'm pregnant again. I told you that I should have gotten those birth control pills! You know that every time the rubber breaks I wind up pregnant! It's alright Dute, I love having a full house with laughter. Sure you do Tom, you only love to make the babies. I just had a baby four months ago. In late October Shirley needed to go to the post office for some stamps so she bundled Linda up and put her in a stroller. She than walked to he post office with Linda and the family dog Lazy.

Shirley decided to leave Lazy and Linda out side of the post office while she went to get her stamps. A few minutes later Shirley came out of the post office and discovered a photographer from the Today's Sunbeam taking pictures of Linda and Lazy. The next day Shirley bought the News paper and found the picture of Linda and Lazy. Under the caption the words read, " A boy and his dog." Shirley thought how in the hell could you not tell that the baby was not a boy. She had on a pink snow suit and black Patten leather shoes. Over the years Tom and Shirley did laugh about this many times.

1964: Tom and Shirley started to look for a house to purchase. After a few months of looking they did find a recently built home on Penn Beach in Pennsville. After carefully going over the family finances Tom went ahead and bought that new house on Harvard road.

Shirley dreaded moving, especially since she was having the same type of pregnancy as her last four. Her legs were swollen and she was feeling miserable. Tom's sister Eva Davis did come to help Shirley to fix up the house. Eva, thank you for helping me put away all of those boxes and fixing up the rooms. Eva I know this is rough on you too. You do have four kids. I know Shirley, I'm glad that I'm not pregnant again!

Jimmy does like keeping me busy. Eva and Shirley both laughed. I hope that you will be staying for dinner? Are you sure you have enough for all of us? I think we should, is two pounds of spaghetti enough for twelve of us? It should be Shirley. I think you guys will be spending the night with us. It looks like Jimmy nor is Tom in any condition to drive. They always find some reason to celebrate! Both women laughed as Shirley served up the dinner.

July 1964, Shirley was in her ninth month of pregnancy. She was feeling miserable she was hallucinating and had yellow jaundice. Dr. Atlig informed her that if she did not give birth soon he would have to perform a cesarean. Mrs. Phillips, your life and the life of your baby is in jeopardy. As the next week came around Shirley was feeling much pressure. I know the baby is coming, so don't get undressed tonight. Dute, you have a ways to go.

You are going to have that baby in August. When he went to bed he went to bed as usual in his under shorts and tee shirt. A couple hours later Shirley woke up. Tom, Tom! We have to go now. Groggy, Tom said now I'm sleeping. No, Tom now! If you were not still drunk from that house warming party we had last night you would understand that I am in labor! Let's go mister! I'm going to have this baby on the floor if we don't go right now!

Doctor Atlig here I am. Mrs. Phillips I am really glad to see you. It does seem however that you always pick the hour that I would be getting my nap. While the doctor examined Shirley he said you are going to give birth soon. Will my baby be alright? You know doctor since I had the toxemia? Mrs. Phillips I need you to push.

With in the next hour Shirley was holding her newborn baby girl. Tom, we had another girl. How do you feel about that? Dute I think we should go home and try for a six pack! Tom, the only six pack you'll be getting is from the liquor store. They both laughed. Dute, you know I love kids. No, Tom you like making them. I am telling Dr. Atlig to put me on the pill this time. Dute, I suppose you are right. As our family has grown my paycheck has not. The prices only go up through the roof.

1964, Christmas Day. Having five children in the house meant plenty of presents. The children had so much paper in the house; Shirley forgot to open her gift from Tom. Shirley got angry that the kids made a mess in the house. Dute, don't worry about the trash for now Tom said while laughing. I don't know what is so funny. Shirley was getting angrier. Tom took a huge box out from behind the Christmas tree and said here Dute open up your present.

No, I don't want any fucking new TV we already have one. We can't afford another one. Well the hell with you than Tom said as he threw the box outside. Cheryl went out and brought the box back into the house. She knew just what was in the box. Mom open the box. No Cheryl, you open up the box if you want to. No Mom this is a nice gift from Dad to you.

Still feeling angry Shirley hesitantly opened the box. What in the hell is this? News paper? Look in the bottom Tom said. As Shirley finished clearing the box her eyes widened. What is this? Open it Dute and see what Santa brought you. Shirley opened the small box and what she saw to her surprise was a new wedding and engagement ring set. What is this for? Dute we have been married ten years and your old set is wearing thin. I thought that you would like a new set of rings Dute. Tom, thank you for my rings I love them. Thanks for making me feel like an ass!

Chapter # 19

1965, Tom was working as hard as he could to keep food on the table for his family. The plumbing and heating business was slow and Shirley took on a part-time job at the Penn Theater. The money was barely enough to help out with food. Shirley was doing all she could considering she was taking care of a house and five young children. Especially after having one baby after another.

Linda and Tammy were only thirteen months apart. To Shirley it was like having twins. When one baby would cry the other one would cry too. For the next three years Tom and Shirley struggled to try and pay the bills. Tom's job went out of business forcing Tom and Shirley to sell their dream house. The mortgage was eating up everything they had. Even though back in1964 this house sold for $35,000.00 or $ 75.00 a month.

Many people lost their jobs in the sixties just as today due to war and the economy. Barney what are you doing here? Is that a way to greet your brother? I have some news for you and Tom. My boss owns a farm house in Quinton, it is on Jericho road. He said that he will rent it to you for $35.00 a month. The house is big. It is a hell of a lot cheaper than this one. When can we see it? How about tonight sis? When they arrived at the farm house Shirley said, Tom looks at the yard and the barn. The house looks big. I said it was sis. Barney thanks for showing us this house. I can't believe that it has four bedrooms a huge living room a kitchen and look at the attic. Plenty of storage. We'll take it.

1967: Tom I received some bad news today. What is going on? Mom called and said that Uncle Frank passed away today. Pack your bags Dute! We have to take a trip to Montrose. Frank's funeral went on for days. After the funeral there was a dinner at Frank's house.

Tom was standing in the living room and said Dute I have always wondered what was in this desk. As kids we were forbidden to touch it. Now there is no one here and I am not a child anymore, I think I should take a peek inside. Tom, don't even think about it. About what? You know Tom. Don't open that desk drawer. Why not? There is no one here. Just than Tom opened the drawer. What is this book? Let's take a look at it. I told you that something was strange about Frank Jr. I can't believe my eyes, this page explains a lot. What does it say? It is a story about the Lindbergh baby.

Than there is a letter here that says that Frank Jr. was adopted just around the time that Charles Lindbergh's baby was kidnapped. Tom, you always make up stories! No, Dute not this time. This paper is from the orphanage that Aunt Peony used to work at. It says that Frank Jr. is the Lindbergh baby. Tom, you know they found that baby dead. Not according to this. Tom, just put that book back in the desk. Someone is coming. Tom and Shirley never spoke much about what they saw in that desk but he later told his kid's all about the book and the letter he read on the day of Frank's funeral.

In the Spring 1968: Tom was doing some plumbing and heating work for himself when one evening he decided to stop at Smitty's Café a local bar in the City of Salem. While drinking a few beers Tom struck up a conversation with the owners of the café. Benny, your bartender just mentioned that you are heater problems, would you like me to look at it? Tom, it is Tom. Yes sir. I will see what my brothers Robbie and Dave say. Can I call you? Here is my number. I'll call to let you know tomorrow afternoon.

The next afternoon Benny Smith did call Tom to let him know that he was going to give him a chance. After looking at the heater Tom thought that the heater was not too bad it only needing cleaning, a filter and a nozzle. The Smith brother's were very satisfied with Tom's work. Do you know how to Bartend? I can do just about everything Benny. Would you like a job working for us? The hours are four to twelve Monday through Saturday. You can do some sideline work for us in our houses when we need repairs if you want to make extra money.

We own a bunch of houses that need repair from time to time. Benny smiled when he saw that Tom looked like he was interested in being a hard worker.

1969: Living in Quinton was very interesting. Tom bought the kids ducks and chickens. He even bought two pigs. Living in the country Tom thought was good and safe for his family. There were many riots going on in the cities. People seemed to be fighting about race and weather the War in Vietnam was of a good cause. Tom usually worked in Smitty's for the 4pm to 12pm shift except for this one day in particular. Tom had to work in the morning. All of the children were in school except for the youngest girl Tammy. Tom, it's time to get up.

Alright Dute, Tom said and then went back to sleep. Tammy gathered all of the jump ropes she could find. She snuck into her father's bedroom while her mother was in the kitchen cooking Tom's breakfast. Tammy proceeded to tie Tom's hands and feet to the bed. As Tom did wake up again he called Dute! Who tied me up? It sure in the hell wasn't me. I was in the kitchen.

By this time Tammy had ran upstairs to her bedroom. Tammy, Shirley screamed, get down the here! Tammy went down the stair steps slowly and crying all the way down. What in hell are you crying about? Why did you tie your dad to the bed? Tammy still sobbing said I don't want dad to go to work! Your father has to go to work to take care of you. Don't let me catch you tying anyone up ever again. I will beat your ass if you do that to anyone ever again. Now go up to your room and think about what you have done. I think you need a nap. Tammy was still crying as she climbed the endless stairs up to her room. Daddy please don't go to work please.....!!!

Many different things happened when the Phillips's lived in the farm house. For example, Tom came home from Smitty's Café after having a little too much to drink. He came into the back door and started chasing the kids around the house holding a snapper turtle that was dripping blood all over the floors that Shirley had just cleaned. Needless to say Shirley was more than a little mad at Tom. Tom did however make snapper soup from that turtle. He said that it was the best soup he had ever eaten.

Thomas had a female dog named Candy. She was having puppies. Dad, Candy is going to have her puppies in my bed. No she will not have her puppies in your bed. Linda watch and see if she has those puppies in my bed or not. It was winter time and Linda asked Thomas, can I sleep in your room on the heater vent? I'm cold! Yes, just be quiet. Linda stop making that noise. What? I was sleeping. You're doing it again, stop it. No I am not Thomas! It is Candy. Look, Linda Candy is having her puppies in my bed I told you so. Thomas called for his parents to come they in return took the puppies and Candy down stairs and let her finish having her puppies in the kitchen where there was a blanket all ready for her.

Cheryl would sneak her than boyfriend into the house to her bedroom. She would tell the younger kids to play hide and go seek and that the attic was a good place to hide. On one particular evening Tom was working and Shirley was at Bingo Cheryl had the kids playing hide in go seek. Tammy and Linda you go and hide in the attic and than told Thomas to count to a hundred. Thomas was looking for the girls for what seemed to be an hour. When Thomas got to the attic, Cheryl opened the door and told Thomas to look for Linda and Tammy in the attic.

When Thomas went up the stairs Cheryl shut the door making the door stick. Cheryl said to Wilbert her boyfriend, now we can have some fun. I got rid of those babies for a while. They both laughed. Being as little as the children were they couldn't open the door themselves. Shirley came home early from Bingo and caught Cheryl and Wilbert kissing on the couch. What the fuck do you think you are doing? Where in the hell are the kids? They are in bed mom! So who is your friend? This is Wilbert. We have been seeing each other for a while now. Wilbert, I think you should go and Cheryl go to your room. We will deal with this later. Shirley could hear screaming by this time.

The kids Shirley thought to herself, where are they? Shirley went to find Terri sleeping in her bed but no Tammy, Linda or Thomas. Shirley finally could hear them scream, let me out help! We are in here. In the attic! Mom's here, I'll get you out. The door was jammed. Shirley had to push hard to open the door. Mom we thought we were going to die in there. It is so scary, we were in there all night, Thomas said.

You kids go get into bed now; I'm going to take care of your sister! Finally, Thomas, Linda and Tammy quieted down but was not sleeping. They heard their mother screaming and slapping Cheryl even though they were not sure why. The next morning Tom spoke to Cheryl about her actions. I love Wilbert Dad. I have been hiding him in my room because he needs a place to stay. His Mom and Dad kicked him out. I want to meet this Wilbert. I need to find out what kind of person he is. Does that mean that he might be able to live with us?

Wilbert, a tall husky young man stood in the back yard. Mr. Phillips, I'm Wilbert Gandy. It is nice to meet you. Your daughter is so beautiful and I love her! I really need a place to stay. I will help out in any way I can. Do you know plumbing? Wilbert had a weird look on his face. Just kidding, welcome to the family. You can stay here on a trial basis. I don't want any drugs around my kids. No pot, nothing. Do you here me? Yes sir! I do need a job, I am willing to do anything. I think I can help you out with that. I need someone who can learn fast. My heating business is busy. I hope you want to learn plumbing and air conditioning?

To Tom's surprise Wilbert did learn fast. Wilbert was becoming part of the family very quickly. Dute, I've been thinking. We should try to move to Salem. It would be closer to the bar. Gas just keeps getting outrageous. I do most of my work in Salem. That is where I make my money. I could try to rent one of Benny's houses.

Why don't you ask him Tom? It is time to move. We have only had problems with this house. First I am tired of walking to the stream to get water, and I am tired of that landlord not fixing anything when it breaks. Sure you can do it but why should you when you pay rent here. What in the hell is the landlord suppose to do? Only collect rent and become a fat rat!

Chapter #20

Tom do you remember when you ask me about renting one of my houses? Sure, Benny I still would like to rent one of your houses when one becomes available. Tom, you are in luck. I have a house on Sinnickson Street that needs some work. It needs a bathroom and a new heater. Just to let you know there is still an outhouse standing in the backyard. Benny I will be glad to do the work if you help us out with the rent.

Tom, I'll buy a sink, shower and a toilet first thing in the morning. I will have to order the heater and the material for you to put in the heat vents. Thanks Benny when can I bring my wife to see the house? How about tomorrow morning? Good that will give me a chance to talk to her tonight. Why don't you go home early so that you can talk to her before she goes to sleep. That would be better than waiting until twelve thirty. It looks like you know my wife Benny! I know women. I have a wife of my own you know.

What are you doing home so early? Shirley sounded angry. I bet you lost your job. No, Dute I have good news. Well don't keep me waiting, Tom. Shirley looked doubtful. We are moving to Salem. We did talk about this. I know Tom but it has been a couple of months. Dute, Benny came to me tonight and told me about a house on Sinnickson Street. Benny wants me to show you the house tomorrow.

Before we go there I just want to let you know that I will be doing some work to the house before we can move in. It is a hell of a lot better than this place. I have to install a new heating system and also a bathroom. Well what do we have to lose? Let's look at the house Tom. By the way how much is the rent? I'm not sure. I will have to talk to Benny about that. I know we will be getting some rent for free. You know for exchange for my services. Dute, the kids are in school already. We need to get going.

Benny is waiting for us to get the key. Here we are. Yuk, look at the color. It is green. I told you the house needs some work. Since Benny likes my work, he did tell me that I can do whatever I want to do. He will even give us free rent in exchange for any improvements that I do. Well that does seem like a good deal Tom. Dute, this is the living room. It looks much smaller than the Quinton house. It is but It does have three bedrooms. Tom was saying this as they were walking around the house looking at the rooms. Dining room, kitchen, I saw the three bedrooms but where in the hell do you think you will be putting a bathroom?

Shirley was getting angry. I don't want to be all cramped up. Dute, just think about it. We are going to make the dining room into a bedroom for us. That bedroom at the top of the stairs is the largest room upstairs and I have a plan to divide that room in half. Ooh! I see make two rooms out of one. Terri can have one half of the room and the other will be our new bathroom. The middle room will be good for Tammy and Linda than Thomas will have his own room. So where will we put Cheryl and Wilbert? They have been talking about getting their own place. In the meantime they can make a room in the attic.

I guess living here will be better than living without running water and a landlord who will never fix a thing. I will need to get some boxes so I can start packing. Within the next month Shirley went to Salem to enroll the kids in the schools. Tammy was going to the John Fenwick, Terri and Cheryl to the Salem High School. Thomas and Linda were enrolled at the Grant Grammar School.

On this one particular day Thomas ask Linda to go with him to Smitty's. The two sat up on the bar stools acting like adults. Bartender Linda said I need a drink. What kind of drink? Tom said laughing. A highball Thomas said and make one for me too Linda said laughing. Coming right up Tom replied while putting Coca Cola in one glass and Sprite and a cherry in another. Thank you sir, put it on our tabs Thomas said. Than everyone began to laugh. Everyone these two are my children Linda and Thomas. All of the patrons of the bar all came over to the kids to say hello. Within the next few minutes Shirley and Tammy came into the bar to have a soda and to pick up Linda and Thomas and take them home for dinner. Many times in the next couple of years Toms children would visit him at the bar just because Tom was usually working by the time they woke up in the morning.

1972: Dute get the bags packed we are going on a little vacation. Where to Montrose again? No, we are going to Canada. We are going camping for three weeks. Tom, won't you lose your job? No, Dute I won't. I have three weeks off. We will be leaving in the morning. I'm shocked Tom. Usually we go to Montrose or North Carolina. I will get all of the camping equipment ready and you should get all the clothes and whatever else we usually take with us. Everyone was so excited to go.

All of the kids found a place in the station wagon. Mom are we leaving? Terri said. What is Canada like? I don't know. Let's just wait until we get there. Are we all ready to go? Dad we are all here, all five us. I just wished that Wilbert could go with us too. Cheryl, he has to work.

His friend Bobby Patterson will be here to keep him company. Let's get going. It will take us quite awhile to get to Canada. After twelve hours of driving Tom said, we are at the border patrol. Just be cool. Sir what is your business here? I brought my family here for vacation sir. The patrol men shined their flashlights and were looking at the children as they were sleeping. Sorry to awaken your children. Sir, it's alright. They will fall back to sleep. Have a wonderful time in our country. Thank you sir. Tom drove away. Whew! Were lucky that those bastards didn't search the car.

Tom, I know if they would have searched our car they would have found your gun in the glove compartment. I'm sure that those bastards wouldn't understand what I am doing with a gun. Tom, you only have it for protection. We always bring that gun with us on all of our vacations. The Phillips family discovered that many things are different in Canada, including the money. Dad, this is a nice camp ground. Can me and Cheryl go get some French fries? Sure Terri, here is some money. That was not unusual except for the part where the women at the concession stand ask Terri and Cheryl if they wanted vinegar on their fries Cheryl said what? Do you want vinegar on your French Fries? No thanks, I would like Ketchup please. The women laughed, and said what a strange request!

Tom made friends everywhere he went. This one gentleman really didn't talk a lot he only said Aye most of the time. Tammy, Thomas and Linda went swimming and they had these strange worms on them. While taking a shower Linda and Tammy were screaming. It hurts Mom, HELP! Shirley pulled these worms off of the girls although she had a tough time doing it. The next day Tom took his family back to the same lake to find out what was in the water.

Tom began talking to a family whose children were swimming in the water. I'm not letting my kids swim in that water. They got some kind of worms on them yesterday. I told my wife that I think they are leaches! That is what they are. Aye, those leaches will come off easy if you put salt on them. Watch us pour the salt on the leaches. Look and see what they do. The leaches fell right off of his kids as he said they would. Montreal had many beautiful places to see. Tom took his family to a huge park for a cookout. Dute, I'll be back by dinner time. I'm going to explore the caves.

I want to look for gold or maybe I'll find some diamonds. Shirley said laughing sure you will! The hours passed by quickly, where is dad? I don't know Tammy. I want my dad to come back Linda said crying. I don't know where he is. Let's eat without him. If he doesn't come soon we will go back to the camp. Your Dad is alright, he has just lost track of time Shirley was trying not to look as scared as she felt. After all they had never went to Canada before. Just as the family was finishing their food Thomas could see his Dad from a distance.

Mom, there is Dad. Daddy, Daddy we missed you. Where have you been Tom? I was worrying about you. I will never mind, look at these rocks that I got! Yea, Yea, Yea, do you want to eat? I'm as hungry as a bear, and speaking of bears I was kind of attacked by a bear. I am so glad that I decided to bring my gun! I thought that I was never coming back. Me too Tom, me too. How about if we just take it easy tomorrow? Tom, I did want to go and do a little shopping. That is kind of relaxing for me. I like sitting out in the car while you go into the store.

You think you are so funny Tom. I'll take a pound of that Lebanon Bologna, We don't carry that kind of meat Ma'am . Yes you do too, it is right there; Shirley said pointing at the meat case. We call that summer sausage here in Canada. Well in America that is Lebanon Bologna. Yes,

Ma'am, we do have many different ways of saying things than you in The United States do. It was nice meeting you Ma'am. It was nice to meet you also Shirley said.

Tom look at this coffee pot that I bought in that store. You should have seen the many different items in that store. It was nice. This is a very nice coffee pot, Dute. I really like this copper design. It will be a good pot to use over open flame or on the stove at home. That's all you ever think about Floyd! I just love your cooking, Dute! Later that day Tom took his family to a lake where there were water lilies growing.

Dad, watch out Terri said than all the other kids repeated after. It's too late, Mom, Dad fell into the water. What, oh no Tom! I'm ok, I got that water lily that you've been asking me for this entire trip. Tom was laughing by this time. Dute, I hope you are satisfied. Shirley was laughing. I didn't tell you to jump in the lake even though at times I wish you would. Everyone began to laugh.

Wilbert, we're home. How is everything around here? They are good except for one small thing. Tom, why didn't you tell me about the liquor that was in the refrigerator? What are talking about? Bobby and I thought that we were drinking water! That's not water! Tom what in the hell was it. Wilbert it was moonshine! Moonshine, so that's why we got so drunk? Do you remember when I had you get rid of the batch of moonshine when we lived in Quinton? I guess I do. Those pigs were so drunk. Tom, I forgot. I hope you pay better attention in the future.

Pop I will try to stay out of trouble. Next time I hope to go on vacation with the family. Wilbert, I think that is a good idea. I believe that is the only way for you to stay out of trouble I have to watch after you twenty four hours a day. Tom, I'm not all that bad, am I? Tom just laughed.

Chapter #21

The Phillips family traveled a lot in the 1970s. Tom built a camper out of an old school bus that he bought from the First Assembly of God Church in Mannington. Frank Bosco, whom Tom did a lot of plumbing and heating for at the time had Tom do some work at the church. For payment Tom did the work at the church in exchange for the bus. The bus was painted a light blue. It had all of the amenities of the RV's you buy today. Some of the places that they traveled were North Carolina, Tennessee, Ohio, Indiana Virginia, Pennsylvania just to name a few.

During the times that they went to North Carolina, Tom would take his family camping in Cherokee on the Indian Reservation. Tom was always recognized by the people in Cherokee and had always been thought of as family. Speaking of family, Tom's sister Eva was living in Waynesville, North Carolina. Since by this time Eva had divorced her husband Jimmy Davis after many years of abuse and alcoholism. Eva had met a very kind and gentle man named Bill who seemed to love and respect Eva and her five children. Any time Tom and Shirley went to North Carolina they made it a tradition to visit Eva.

In 1977 Shirley and Eva were having a conversation about a surgery that Eva had on her gallbladder. Shirley, don't I look pregnant? Shirley nodded yes. The doctor told me that I only needed my gallbladder removed. That is why he had said I was bloated. I was told by him that I had a severe infection. A couple days after my surgery, the doctor came into my hospital room telling me that he had some news for me about my condition. Shirley I never dreamed in a million years what he was going to tell me. He said Eva you have CANCER! What? Shirley replied. Can the doctor's do anything for you? No, Eva said trying to hold back the tears. The cancer doctor says that I only have about a year to live. While in surgery the doctor's took out about this much of my bowel.

Eva was holding out her hands about six or seven inches apart. They say I must have had this cancer for quite a while. Choking back the tears, Shirley said Eva if I or Tom can help in any way just call us. There is nothing anyone can do except pray. Could you please tell Mom and Dad about my cancer? Not that they will care anyway. Eva was estranged from Floyd and Anna. I will probably not see them again at least while I'm alive. Eva, I am so sorry that Mom and Dad act the way they do to you. Tom and I will talk to them for you. You know that we do love you. I love you and my brother more than words can say.

I am glad that I had a chance to tell you about the cancer without Tom here. Now with your help and support I can tell him myself. Eva sat down with Tom at her kitchen table to tell him about the cancer. She told him how she wanted her children cared for and how she felt that Tom would make sure that Floyd and Anna would know how much she still needed and loved them.

1978: Cancer treatment was so expensive and most treatments were experimental that Eva really could not afford the treatment. On the first Sunday after Tom came home from North Carolina he went to dinner at Anna and Floyd's house. Tom you're early. Anna was sitting in the kitchen peeling potatoes. What's wrong Tom. Ma I have something to tell you about Eva.

Tom, what did I tell you before? I don't want to talk about anything that has to do with that family! They are nothing but trash and bad news! Ma, wait a fucking minute! Eva is sick, she has cancer! She only has a year to live. She is dying from the same kind of cancer that killed Uncle Matt. Mom, don't you care? Tom couldn't talk to his mother any longer. Dute, let's go home! Tom was not used to fighting with his parents and he didn't know how to make them understand that all he wanted for Eva was to have their parents to say the three words I love you and I'm sorry.

Tom knew deep down inside that this was not going to happen but he was going to try and make amends to his parents as soon as he cooled off. Over the next year and a half or so Tom and Shirley visited Eva in North Carolina as much as they could.

1979: This is saddest trip we have ever taken to North Carolina, Tom. I know Dute. It doesn't feel right visiting a nursing home for a person that is only forty two years old. After inside the nursing home the staff was friendly and seemed to care about the patient's best they could. Hi, I'm Shirley and this is my husband Tom. We are looking for Tom's sister Eva Davis. She is right down here. The nurse led the way to her room. She is in the bed on the left. Enjoy your visit.

When Tom entered the room he noticed that Eva was frail. She had dropped from one hundred twenty pounds to sixty pounds. She looked like a skeleton with skin. Eva was in good spirits when she saw Tom at the foot of her bed. Tom it is so good to see you. It is good to see you too Eva. Shirley I sure could go for a beer! That was strange coming from Eva since she didn't drink beer. I'll bring you one tomorrow. Thanks Shirley.

Tom and Shirley talked with Eva for a few hours. They talked about their childhood, their parents and all the things that Eva thought she was going to miss. Eva, Shirley and I will see you tomorrow. You need your rest. By this time, Eva was groggy from the Morphine Drip. Mr. Phillips the Nurse said, I would like to talk to you about your sister. Sure, could my wife sit in the room with us? She is welcome too if she would like. Mr. Phillips. Call me Tom. Tom, you know that your sister is very ill. Yes Tom nodded. She is having Chaney stokes breathing.

You may or may not know that is when a person stops breathing and then starts breathing again. Yes I have seen that before. I did see Eva do that too. I know she is dying. How long does she have? Your sister has as much as a few days. It will be soon. I know that Eva ask you for beer. Beer is forbidden in this Nursing home but at this time all we care about is Eva's comfort, so you can bring all the beer you want. Thank you nurse. I am sorry about your sister Tom; she is a very nice lady. Thank you.

Call us at the number we gave you if there are any changes. I will Mr. Phillips. Take care. Tom's other sister Josephine found Tom at the campground. Tom how is she? Not good Josephine. We are going back to see her tomorrow if you want to go with Dute and me to Waynesville. What time are you planning to go to the Nursing Home? Probably around nine. Is that alright. Yes, I'll probably be up all night anyway.

Me too. Why don't you stay up and have some coffee with me? I could do that.

The next morning without any sleep Tom, Shirley and Josephine went to the Nursing Home carrying a case of Budweiser Beer. Eva, how are you today? Tom asks. I think that God has it in for me. Eva tried to crack a smile. Did you bring me my beer? What do you think this is? A Suitcase? I have the beer right here Josephine said. I think I'll have a couple with you. Don't forget about your brother. I will never forget about you or Josephine. I love you both. We love you too, Tom and Josephine both said. I love you too Eva, Shirley also said.

The three stayed with Eva for the entire day knowing that she only had days or hours left to live. Two o'clock in the morning the owner from the Cherokee Campground knocked on the Mobile home door. Mrs. Phillips your husband has a telephone call in the office. It is a Nurse from Waynesville is on the phone. I'll get my slippers on. Could you tell them I'll be right there? Yes, Ma'am I will. Tom I have to get the phone. I'll be right back. Hello, is this Mrs. Phillips? Yes it is. This is the charge Nurse, I'm Calling from the Nursing home about Eva Davis. Yes. Eva is not doing well. To be honest with you she may only have hours to live. She is asking for her brother Tom. Thank you for calling. We will be there as soon as we possibly can. Thank You Mrs. Phillips, we will expect to see you soon.

Shirley hung up the phone trying to hold back the tears that were evident in her eyes. As Shirley reached the Mobile home she saw Tom standing in the door smoking a cigarette. What was that call about? It is you sister, we have to go. Eva is not doing well. Tom, Shirley and Josephine took that sad ride down the Great Smokey Mountains to Waynesville not sure what to expect next. Again at the nursing home Tom stopped to talk to the charge nurse. Hello, Mr. Phillips. How is my sister? She has taken a turn for the worse. She may not make it through the night. Thank you for calling us Tom said. Are we all allowed to sit with her? Yes, go right on into her room. All three went into the room slowly. As Eva awoke she said to them Hi. I'm glad to see you (She was gasping for breath)

Tom please make sure my kids are taken care of, especially Dawn. I really don't know what she will do without me. Please get her out of that foster home. Don't worry Eva we will take care of everything. With tears in Eva's eyes she said I don't want to die but god said it is my time.

I'm in so much pain. I'm afraid to leave my family, I will miss you all. Eva was crying and she was Cheney Stoking more now than before.

Eva we will miss you too and we all love you more than words can say Tom said with tears in his eyes. Even though we will feel sorrow and strife we know that god needs you right now in his kingdom. It is alright to close your eyes and let god take charge of your life. Tom's voice was choking. The nurse came into the room to check on Eva's vital signs and she pushed the pump so that the Morphine would go into Eva's veins faster now. Tom stepped out of the room to talk to the nurse. I want to thank you for all you did for my sister.

I know that she is fading fast. Mr. Phillips would you like me to call the priest to give to her the last rights? Yes I would like if you could do that for us. Could we stay with my sister until she is gone? Mr. Phillips most people don't have the opportunity to be with their loved ones when they pass away. You and your family may stay with Eva for as long as you would like. Eva mostly slept. The priest came and prayed with the family and he gave Eva her last rights. With Josephine, Tom and Shirley by Eva's bedside Eva passed away a couple of hours after the priest came to see her. Tom was holding her hand.

Good bye my sister. I will miss you and I love you. Tom than reached down to Eva and kissed her on the cheek. I'll see you again someday in heaven my sweet little sister. Eva's funeral was simple. All of her Brother's and her Sister was there. Anna and Floyd did show up but as expected they never shed a tear. Dawn her ten year old daughter was there but she didn't know what was going on exactly. At ten years old it is hard to understand that your only caretaker is gone forever. Eva's sons Jimmy, Bobby and Jay came to the funeral wearing blue jeans.

Cathy the oldest daughter could not make the trip from California. She could not afford the airline ticket to come back east. When Tom and Shirley went to look at Eva in the casket they said to each other how cheap. The casket was light blue and it looked like a cardboard box. Shirley and her children went all out to buy Eva a White Silk Nightgown and matching Robe. Eva had told Shirley that she wanted a fancy night gown when she died. There were plenty of flowers.

The Rafferty family, the "Hillbillies" of North Carolina came to the funeral dressed in old ragged Bib Overall Jeans and Holy Tee-Shirts. Eva was buried in a grave that her sons Bobby and Jimmy had to dig since Floyd and Anna were too cheap to pay for opening the grave. After the funeral was over, Tom and his family went to the Nursing Home and took a couple bouquets of flowers for the patients to enjoy. Nurse, these flowers were left from the Eva Davis funeral.

Could we give them to you for the patients to enjoy? You certainly may. Tom and I would like to thank you and your staff for all of the things you have done for Eva. Thank you for making my sister's last moments as comfortable as you could Tom said with tears in his eyes. Your welcome the charge nurse said. We have packed up Eva's belongings. Do you think that her children could pick up these bags? I could take them to her children if you would like me to. I guess that would be alright. It was a pleasure to take care of your sister. We will all miss her around here. I am going to miss her more than you know.

Tom and Shirley went to see Jimmy, Bobby and Jay to find out if they wanted anything from the two bags. Uncle Tom, I thought you were going home today. We have some of your Mother's things in the Van. Uncle Tom, Mom gave me a note of what she wants us kids to have, Jimmy said. Could you keep the bags for now Uncle Tom? I will take them with me to New Jersey or when you are ready for them you could either pick them up or I will bring them to you the next time I visit.

You are going to still come to see us even though Mom is gone. Sure I will. You are my family Tom said his voice choking up. Take care of yourself. You all take care of each other and call me if you need me. Ok? Bye Uncle Tom. While driving back to New Jersey Shirley said, did you kids open that bag of Eva's? No Mom it's under the bed in the back of the Van where Dad put it.

We are just behind you playing cards. I have to pull over! Something in this Van stinks! Are you sure that Eva's bags are tied? Dad we haven't touched those bags! Tom did stop at the very next rest area. He and Shirley did check to see where the nasty smell was coming from. There was nothing in the Van except for Eva's two bags. I guess the smell of cancer is seeping through those closed bags.

After arriving home from North Carolina Tom and Shirley unloaded all of their belongings including Eva's two bags. Tom, what do you want me to do with these two bags? Just put them in our bedroom Dute. We can go through them later on. It seemed as soon as Eva's bags were placed in the bedroom the smell just disappeared. In the next few months nothing out of the ordinary happened until this one particular evening. Thomas, Linda and Tammy were in their bedrooms. Hey you kids get your asses down here right now!

What's wrong Mom, Thomas said. Have you kids been into Eva's stuff? No each person replied. Look, Mom this bag is tied up tight, Linda said. This other bag is closed up tight Mom, Tammy said. What's going on Mom? This night gown is not mine. It was laying on my bed. This is one of Eva's night gowns! How did this get on my bed? I want answers! Mom, we didn't do this! Linda said. I know that Eva is here. What are you talking about Linda?

I saw Eva sitting on my dresser a few times now. I thought that I was dreaming. She was wearing a white gown and had a bright pinkish, orange haze around her. A color that I've never seen before. She told me that she was here to protect me and that she would help and protect me until the end of my life. Than she was gone, she only spoke to me that one time. Tom than went into the bedroom and saw that the kids and Shirley were now sitting on the bed. I know that Eva came home with us, because the smell went away as soon as we got back to New Jersey. There have been some strange things that has happened to me ever since we have come back home.

Eva if you are listening, Thank you for being my sister and for helping us. Now go and spend some time with God and enjoy Heaven. After that Tom and Shirley opened the bags and went through them. They put the night gown back into one of the bags and then tied them both up. Eva has never come around ever again. Nothing else strange ever happened while the Phillips's lived on Sinnickson Street.

Chapter # 22

1980:   Dute, while I was working in Pennsgrove today, I found a house that I thought we could rent. What are you talking about Tom? It will be a good idea Dute. Since I am working with Jerry it makes sense. I will only have to go to Golf wood Avenue. I will still be working some odd jobs for Benny. I'm sick and tired of this town. Well I guess after living here for nearly twelve years it is time for a change. When Linda, Thomas and Tammy found out, they didn't want to move. Thomas was in his senior year in High School, Linda was a junior and Tammy was a freshman.

Why would you want to move out of this house? It is only sixty dollars a month. They want to pay one hundred fifty dollars for that house, which is a ninety dollar difference. They must be going crazy. I should rent out this house myself and it's only sixty dollars. Linda and Tammy just laughed. While packing Shirley came across some pictures that were let's just say inappropriate for young eyes. Shirley was ripping up the pictures saying sick, sick, sick!

Yea, you weren't saying that when Dad took those pictures Thomas said laughing. You were saying STOP IT TOM! Shirley would often say that when Tom would be suggesting sex. Thomas you'd better shut up before I beat your ass! Shirley was looking embarrassed. Thomas was still chuckling. A month later the Phillips family moved to 39 South Broad Street in Pennsgrove, with the exception of Cheryl and Terri who were married. Cheryl did marry Wilbert Gandy and Terri Married

George Kelly Jr. and as years went on she had a son Joseph, and two daughters Lynne, and Angelia.

By 1980 Cheryl had three children, Kenny, Brian and Bonnie. Terri had one son named Joseph Jr. Since Thomas is in his senior year in Salem he will graduate from there. What about us Tammy said. You and Linda will finish this year in Salem than transfer to Pennsgrove next year. I don't think so Mom! What do you mean Tammy? I don't like Pennsgrove. We went to Salem schools all of this time and now you want us to transfer! I will quit first and get my GED. Me too Linda said.

I will either take the bus to Salem or I will quit and get my GED too! Dute, what in the hell is wrong with you? Those kids are doing alright in Salem. Why do you want to mess up their schooling? We can still use a Salem address. I guess you forgot that Cheryl does live in Salem. I guess you are right. So how will they get back and forth to school every day? Don't you think it'll be a pain in the ass! Dute, everything for you is a pain in the ass! Mom don't forget I have a car.

Thomas, but what about when you go to work? We can take the bus or catch a ride home with you Mom. Linda that sounds like a good idea, Tom replied. Shirley was mumbling under her breath maybe after they take the bus a few times they will want to transfer. That's what she thinks Tammy said. I know I'll graduate from Salem and there is nothing she or anyone else can do about it! We will all graduate from Salem Thomas said. Then, Tammy, Linda and Thomas went out to his car so that they could plan their next move.

McDonalds in Pennsville was the old talking spot when the kids needed to talk and also eat. June came along quickly; Thomas graduated from Salem as planned. Christmas day was always exciting in the Phillips house. The year of 1980 Thomas had been dating Jacqueline Hand. (Jackie) Jackie, will you marry me? Tom and Shirley were excited for Thomas. Jackie had been a family friend for many years. They knew that she would be a very good wife for Thomas.

Of course Thomas did say at three years old that he was going to marry her some day. Well someday did come in May of 1981. Thomas and Jackie got married in the First Assembly of God Church in Pennsville. The Reverend William Edward Tackett officiated. He was a very good friend to Linda who knew him as Ed. The wedding reception was held in the Democrat Club at that time it was on Churchtown Road in Pennsville.

June of 1981, Linda did graduate from Salem High School as she planned. Tammy also graduated in 1983 from Salem. Ha, Ha, We did graduate from Salem as we planned! They thought we'd never pull it off. I guess we fooled them. Yea Tammy, we really pulled it off. What kind of idiots do they think we are any-way? Tammy and Linda just laughed! After Tammy graduated from High School, Tom decided to buy another house in Salem on Yorke Street.

The house only cost him seven thousand dollars. It was a good deal. Benny Smith had many houses and Tom decided that at seven thousand dollars this house was a good investment. The house needed a little tender loving care. Tom had put up new paneling, kitchen cabinets, carpeting and anything else that the house needed. We are not moving again Linda said. So where are you are going to live? Me and Tammy can afford to pay rent on this house. I'm not moving back to Salem right now. I have a job and a car. You two will move out. Tammy and Linda just laughed because they knew that at the time their boyfriends would stay with them and help them out.

Tammy was dating Agapito Correa and Linda was dating Jose' Santiago. After about a year Jose' and Linda moved to Massachusetts and Tammy and Agapito did move into the Yorke Street house with Tom and Shirley. January of 1985. Mom it's me Linda. I was calling to tell you and Dad that I'm pregnant. I have decided to stay here in Massachusetts. Jose' got a good job in Cambridge. I'm glad for you. Tell Jose' that we said hello and to take care of you.

After a couple of months, Linda and Jose' moved out of his Mother's house on Spruce street in Lawrence. They only moved to the next house over. The third floor apartment at this time was the only one in Jose's budget of two hundred dollars. Jose', look my Mom and Dad are here. They didn't tell me that they were coming. What a surprise. Mom, Dad I'm glad to see you! What is this? It's a bassinet for the new baby! Wow, look at all the gifts! Mom this is wonderful. Linda had gotten almost everything that she needed for her baby. Dute, I'll be right back, I'm going to the truck to get something.

When he returned he said God damn! This place must be loaded with roaches! What do you mean by that Tom? Jose', When I opened my glove compartment about a million of those cock suckers flew out.

I thought I was being attacked! Dad I guess you'll need some spray. Linda, I need more like a bomb to get rid of those bastards! They are monster bugs. I've seen roaches, but those roaches are as big as cars! Everyone began laughing.

September 20, 1985: Shirley this is Jose', Linda has had the baby, it's a girl. Tom and Shirley left New Jersey to go to Lawrence to see Linda and her new daughter. Upon arriving at the Lawrence General Hospital Shirley said I'm tired. I hope that they let us in. It is past visiting hours. Jose' said they will let us in to see Linda. He already told the nurses to expect us. How may I help you the receptionist at the front desk said? We came here to see my daughter.

We have driven six hours from New Jersey. Yes Ma'am, I will call the Nurses station to see if they are going to let you up to maternity. Go on up. They said they were expecting you. Thank you Tom said. Mom, what are you doing here? I didn't want to wait until morning. So where is my granddaughter? Dad she is in intensive care Linda said sadly. Why? What happened? She had the umbilical cord wrapped several times around her neck. The doctors have said that the first twenty four house are critical and that she may not make it. I'm going down to intensive care to see her. Dad, you don't have to bother right now. I'm going down to talk to her and to God. So what did you name her? Mom, Jose' and I have been fighting about that.

I like Victoria and he likes Teresa. I settled for Monica. Oh like in General Hospital. Right, I saw an episode today with Monica and I had never thought about pretty the name was. We threw a few names around and came up with Monica Lydia Santiago. That's pretty. Tom, so what did you find out? She has tubes everywhere. God will take care of her. Don't worry. What did I miss while I was gone? Just that the baby is Monica. I saw that on her card.

Linda, how would you like to see your baby? Nurse I don't want to see her sick. I can't take the pain of losing her. No you don't understand, your baby is doing wonderful. She is a miracle. We are still going to monitor her but she is being moved to the regular nursery. Linda's eyes filled with tears of joy. Mom and Dad, I heard people saying that I was in a private room because my baby died. Now I can prove them wrong.

1987: Tom and Shirley visited Massachusetts many times in the past couple of years. Dute, look at this ad; they are looking for a handy man at this motel in South Lawrence. It sounds like a good job! What are you crazy? Do you think we are going to move to Massachusetts? Why not? I'm sick of Salem anyway. Floyd, I'm not going to move up here! Well Dute you can just stay in New Jersey all by yourself. I guess you are right. With all the kids grown there is nothing holding us back. We should give it a try. Dute that is what I'm talking about. Tom, I called about the job. It sounds good; Mr. Kady said that there is an apartment that comes with the job.

We will meet with him tomorrow. The next day Tom and Shirley went to meet Arthur Kady. Tom, your credentials are impeccable. You have got the Job. When can you start Mr. Phillips? We will be here the first of the month. Is that alright with you? That will be perfect. See you next month. Tom and Shirley you may call me Art. See you soon Art. So Mr. Smarty pants, what in the hell are we going to do with the house? And what about the furniture? Have a yard sale and sell what you don't want. Terri wants to rent the house from us. I guess that is a good idea. At least the house will be with someone we can trust. Dute, I really don't care about the house anyway.

For all I care I could take a match to it! Oh Tom just stop it. You always think I'm kidding just like you thought that I was kidding the time I stuffed those guys in the trash cans that were full of glass! I fucked them up! And why not? Nobody calls my wife a Whore! Tom, you like to fight when you are drunk! Yes, I was at McCarthy's Bar drinking but, I was not loaded Dute! I know that those men called you a Whore and I defended you. I may have gotten carried away; you know going back there with a gun and all. If it wasn't for Benny's Philly Lawyer friend you could have gone to jail for attempted murder. Dute that was so long ago, the past is the past.

Look into my crystal ball. What do you see? Tom, you think you are so funny. Answer my question Dute. I see trouble. Why, I don't drink much anymore. Yea but sometimes your temper could get you in trouble. You don't know the cops the way you do here in Salem. You are lucky that back in the seventies when you took that gun and shot holes into the boat you didn't get caught! Dute that was my boat until those thieves stole it. I just figured that if I couldn't have it than nobody should have it and that's why it sits in the bottom of the Salem river right now as we speak. I am glad that we are getting out of this town. I'm finally glad that you see it my way Dute!

Chapter #23

Tom pulled up to the Motel with his truck loaded to the top. Jose' was there to help out. Before you knew it some people from the motel were helping Tom and Shirley unload the truck. One person who was living in the motel at the time was Jose's uncle Carlos who helped in organizing the men who unloaded the truck and was introducing Tom as his good friend.

Carlos did know Tom from the Santiago parties he had attended. Tammy and Agapito also had a daughter in December of 1985. Agapito also was one of the people who helped Tom and Shirley get settled into their new home. Pito as Tom knew him had moved to Massachusetts to find a job. Tammy had stayed in New Jersey waiting for Pito to bring her and Ashley to Massachusetts. Around November Tammy did finally get an apartment with Pito. They moved to Saratoga Street.

January 1988: Massachusetts was cold and snowy. The job at the motel was going pretty good. For the most part the Phillips's were happy. Tom your Mom is on the phone. What is going on Ma? Tom we need you to come home to New Jersey. It's Pop. His kidneys are failing! The doctor says that he is dying. Alright Ma, I'll be leaving in the morning. See you Ma. Tell Pa that I am on my way. The phone rang in the wee hours of the morning. Tom Anna said crying, Pop is gone. I'm on my way Ma, I love you. Dute, my Dad died. I should have gone last night when Ma first called. Now it's too late I can't even say goodbye. Tom's tears were flowing.

I will never forget the day of January 4th for as long as I live. Floyd's funeral was held in Ashcraft Funeral Home in Pennsgrove and he was laid to rest in the Sharp Town Cemetery. Soon after Floyds funeral Linda found out that she was pregnant with her second child. Jessica Ann Santiago was born October 11, 1988. Tom really did not talk about his father much after his death. One thing that was for sure Anna talked a lot about how Floyds Mother was Mexican. That was why a lot of Floyds family did not speak to each other.

There was a lot of controversy about Floyd's father coming from Whales, England. He went out west to Texas to help build the rail road and he soon fell in love with a young Mexican women named Nina'. Her family was not happy about the union and of course Floyd's father coming from England his family was not happy just the same. So his family split up and went in all kinds of directions. Floyd's mother and father moved to Montrose, PA. Together they did have several kids. One who was also named Nina', Floyd, and Arthur just to name a few.

Tom was emotionally drained by the time he went back home. Dute, could you please call Josephine and ask her to go to Cheryl and see if she could go to Ma's house to help out for awhile? Tom, I've already taken care of that. She is there already. Cheryl was one of Anna's favorite grandchildren. Since she was her very first. Anna was still very saddened with the death of Floyd. Tom did go to New Jersey to visit his mother as much as he could. On this one particular trip Anna said to Tom, I keep on having Diarrhea! I can't stop! Ma you need to go to see Doctor Harris.

You have lost weight! No thanks to your kids I was very fat! Now thanks to your Pop I am thin. Anna laughed. Ma you are too skinny. You are not eating! I am too! I eat like a cow! Tom noticed that Anna was only eating a very little off of a sandwich plate. Ma I am going to take you to Doctor Harris tomorrow. Anna finally agreed. In the next month Doctor Harris had hospitalized Anna for various tests. When the test results came back Doctor Harris did not have good news to tell Anna. Anna I'm going to tell you straight. Your test results show that you have cancer.

Anna had tears in her eyes. So what are we going to do about the cancer Doctor? I'm afraid Anna that the cancer has spread throughout your body including your bowels. I just knew that I had bowel cancer! We will make you as comfortable as possible. I will give you the best care that I can. Doctor Harris said this knowing that Anna would not live much longer. Her body was already so frail. A few days after the doctor told Anna about the cancer she took a turn for the worst. Doctor Harris was a great friend to the Phillips family and he called her family himself.

He told them to prepare for the worst. Tom, oh hi John, how are you? I'm fine but Ma is not doing so well, John said with a choke in his voice. She is dying! We need you to come as soon as possible. She is in Elmer Hospital. I'll be there as quickly as I can. I will leave as soon as Dute packs. Tom, what's wrong? It's Ma, she is dying let's go to New Jersey. What about the Hotel? I'll have to stay here. The hell you will. I'm not going to miss saying goodbye to my mother! I missed saying goodbye to my dad. Now get our bags packed! I'll call Art and let him know that we have an emergency! If he don't like it he can go to hell!

Tom and Shirley arrived in Elmer at around four o'clock P.M. Ma, I'm here! Anna's eyes filled with tears. She couldn't talk because she had tubes coming out of her everywhere. Tom said in a choking voice, I love you Ma. Anna's tears were flowing. Tom and Shirley stayed with Anna for the entire day. Before leaving Tom said this prayer. Lord we ask you to keep my mother safe in your arms. We know that she loves you and that you have called her home. In Jesus name we pray, Amen.

June 13th 1990: Tom, Shirley, John and Ruthanne sat by Anna's bedside and watched her slip away from this world and into heaven. The hour was bitter sweet. Tom was very distraught as were all of her children. Anna's house was quiet that evening. Linda and Tammy had traveled that terrible trip from Massachusetts to New Jersey. One strange thing did happen though. Tammy and Linda did get to New Jersey in four hours. It is usually a six to eight hour trip. What, you're here already? Did you fly? No Mom, you wouldn't believe it if you hear it.

Tammy and I were driving near Hartford Connecticut, When Tammy said to me two more hours to New York. I said well I guess we should flip a coin to see who drives through New York. That was always a joke that Tammy and Linda would say to each other before driving through the horrid traffic in New York. The next thing we knew we had by passed most of Connecticut, and were at the toll both in the beginning of New Jersey getting our ticket. Tammy said don't you think it's weird? Oh come on! Mom, we're not lying, it really happened! Linda and Tammy both said. Tom trying to smile said Whew, it sounds like the twilight zone! On that note everyone just laughed and never talked about the incident again with the exception of Tammy and Linda who talk about it often. Anna's house always had a weird vibe.

Tammy and Linda tried to sleep, on the pullout couch and Shirley and Tom were upstairs in one of the bedrooms that they had shared in the early years. Did you hear that? Tammy you mean the chair scraping on the kitchen floor? Check it out! No, Linda you check it out. I'll go if you go. Tammy and Linda walked through the dining room to the kitchen; I wonder who moved Grand Mom's chair out? I don't know but I'm not staying out here to find out. Mom, Tammy and Linda said. Come down here, Mom! What's wrong? Grand Mom's green chair is pulled out from the table and coffee has been made. Were you just down here? Tammy said.

No, I was sleeping until you called me to come down here. How about Dad? He is sleeping. You know he hasn't had much sleep. Just unplug the coffee pot and go the hell back to bed! Tammy I don't know about you but I'm not going to the kitchen for a while, especially by myself. Me either! I can't wait to leave this haunted house! Tammy said it has always freaked me out! Me too sister, me too. Tammy and Linda stayed up all that evening talking about their grandmother and the past.

In the morning Shirley made everyone breakfast. It feels weird sitting here without Ma and Pop here Tom said. I would like to pray. Lord we come to you today to thank you for your blessings, (Tom's voice was choking up) and the gifts you give to us every day. We don't understand what you do or why you do it but our faith and lives are always with you. We thank you for our food we say all of this in Jesus name we pray, Amen. Tom had to leave the table, his tears were flowing and he was not one to let anyone see his tears. After breakfast was over Tom was looking in the Bible.

What do you think about the book of Ecclesiastics, Chapter three? What's on your mind Tom's brothers said. You know the verse that talks about everything has a reason or a season? Listen to me. To everything there is a season a time for every purpose under heaven. A time to be born a time to die. A time to plant a time to pluck which has been planted. A time to kill and a time to heal. A time to breakdown and a time to build up. A time to weep and a time to laugh. A time to mourn and a time to dance. A time to cast away stones and a time to gather stones. A time to embrace and a time to refrain from embracing. A time to gain and a time to lose. A time to keep an a time to throw away. A time to tear and a time to sew. A time to keep silent and a time to speak. A time to love and a time to hate. A time for war and a time for peace.

Don't you think that Ma would like this? Tom said to his brothers and his sister Josephine. They were all letting the tears flow freely now. Anna was dressed in red pants and a white blouse and red vest. This outfit was considered the Cooties club dress code. She had lady bug pins that decorated her vest, the symbols of the Cooties. Anna had many flowers and her casket was a light blue in color. There were many people at Anna's funeral. She and Floyd had made many, many friends over the years since they had moved from Montrose.

Chapter # 24

1991: Art had decided to sell the hotel where Tom and Shirley had been working. Hello, Jerry how have you been doing? I'm fine. What's on your mind Tom? I was wondering if that offer still stands. So do you want to come and live in Delaware? Carl King is still hiring. Tom, I'll call them tomorrow and make sure if they could use you. I don't see why not you are a great heater and air conditioner man. Dute and I are ready to move. I'll call you back tomorrow. So Dute it is up to you now. I either go back to work for Benny or we move to Delaware.

Jerry says that the job with Carl King does pay pretty good. You won't have to work. That I like. See Dute it might be a good change. When are we going? How about the end of January? Jerry did say that they needed someone as soon as possible. Tom, I'm ready to go right now. Tom and Shirley did move to this cute little house in Camden Delaware. Tom this house is a little small. I know but we only need one bedroom we are only two people.

We can use one bedroom for us and the other one for our extra stuff. We wouldn't need the extra space if you were not such a pack rat Tom! Tom and Shirley soon found out that the house that they were living in was an old church. And when they would sleep forget about it! The train would always shake the house whenever it came down the tracks.

Spring 1993: Dute I think that we should move out of this train car! Tom, I hate to move. The mobile home that I am talking about is much bigger than this train car. Let's go look at it tonight. That evening Tom and Shirley went to see the mobile home. This looks nice. I hate to tell you I told you so! Look, we have three bedrooms, living room, dining room, kitchen and bath. What a nice country setting. The carpet needs cleaning. Dute, we can clean the carpet or get new carpet. Do you want to move here or not? I don't know if I do Tom!

You said that you were tired of that little house. No, I'm tired of MOVING! Tom spent many days sitting by the window looking at the humming birds flying around outside. When on this one particular day Tom saw something strange. Dute guess what I saw today? I don't know. I saw what looked like ghost out there in the field. They looked like they were floating. Tom, what are you on? Dute I am telling you they were ghosts who were dressed like people from the eighteen hundreds. I can prove it. Just wait until I get the pictures developed. You took pictures? Not believing what Tom was saying. Dute, seeing is believing, but you don't always see what you believe. I know that I saw what I saw. Tom never did get the film developed. So, who knows what he saw in that field.

1994: Shirley was working for a dry cleaning service named Capitol Cleaners. Tom, they need someone to drive around picking up the clothes. This would be an easier job than the one you were doing for Carl King! Dute, you know that I have been having leg problems! That is why Tom stopped working for the heating company. I do need to take it easy. The doctors at the Lawrence General Hospital told you that with the deep vein Thrombosis you should watch what you are doing.

I like those doctors in Massachusetts! Sometimes I think that we should have stayed living there. Tom went on to work for the cleaners. He had a route in which he would go to Rehoboth Beach every night. On one of Linda's visits to Delaware she had ask Tom if she could go with him on his run this one evening. Dad, why don't I go with you tonight?

I guess you can if you want to. Mom said that your legs are bothering again. They are kind of painful. So I can go with you? Yes! While driving from the Harrington store Tom stopped in a hurry. Dad! What's wrong? Are you in pain? No there is a dime over there. Tom got out of the van and bent over to pick up a dime. Dad, you are crazy! If I left that dime there than some other vulture would come along and pick it up. Tom often would stop on the highway to pick up money or tools that he would see. He had hawk eyes. Linda was just laughing to herself.

1998: Tom finally decided to retire. Dute, I saw an RV that old man Ford is selling. So what are you telling me for? I have asked Thomas to call to Ford Flowers for the price. You know that it would be nice for us to travel. We are both retired now. Dute, you know that I've wanted a Camper since the old days when I turned that Bus into a Camper. Tom, all you do is dream. So what is so wrong with dreaming? Thomas, so how much is the camper?

Dad, Mr. Ford wants twenty five hundred dollars for it. That's not bad. Could you go down and give him some money to hold it until this weekend? Sure Dad, so you are coming to New Jersey this weekend? Yes, we will be there by noon! The RV needed some fixing up but all in all it was a very good deal. Tom was out day and night fixing up that camper. One evening Shirley went to talk to Tom. She saw smoke. What is he doing she thought to herself. Tom, what are you doing? I'm working on the camper!

No, I mean what are you doing with that Cigarette in your mouth? I'm smoking it! Tom, you stopped smoking for nearly ten years! So, Dute, you only live for so many years so why not die happy? You sound like that lady at the Social Security office. What about her? Remember when she ask me for my ID and I gave her my social security card and my driver's license?

Yes! Well she asks me if I really was Floyd Matthew Phillips. Do you remember what I said to her? No! I said, it was me when I looked in the mirror this morning! She had the dumbest look on her face. Tom was now laughing. That bitch told me I looked too young to be Floyd. I told her that I was Tom and Floyd was my alter ego! She got pissed off by then. Shirley began laughing.

Chapter # 25

May 1998: Forty Eight years after the Korean war, Jerry was honored at a Memorial day service for his bravery in Korea. The service took place in the Camden, Delaware VFW. Jerry was awarded the Purple Heart, the Korean Service Metal, United Nations Service Metal, the National Defense Service Metal, and the Good Conduct Metal. After the ceremony Jerry had a cook out at his home in Dover, Delaware to Celebrate.

October 1998: Hello, Oh, hi Ruthanne, I have bad news Ruthanne was choking back the tears. John died! What! I said John died! What happened? He was sleeping, and he didn't wake up. Our daughter Kim found him. She went into our bedroom to put away some clothes. She said Dad must be cold. His feet are purple. Then I checked him he was not breathing. I'll call you back with the funeral information. Thanks for calling Ruthanne, I'll tell Tom. Dute what's wrong? Shirley was crying. Tom its John he's dead!

I overheard some of your conversation; I can't believe that my baby brother is dead! How could this happen? Tom I remember him saying at the Rafferty family reunion that he was having a lot of heart burn and had a weird fluttering in his heart. That is signs that someone could possibly have Heart problems. I wished it was me Dute, and not my brother who was only forty seven years old. John had a memorial service with a viewing. He was later cremated and was buried in the same plot where Anna, Floyd and his son John are buried.

1999: Spring couldn't come fast enough for Tom. He and Shirley were finally going to do some traveling. Tom, how in the hell do you think we can travel with our Social Security checks and pay rent here? We are going to move our stuff into storage and live in the RV. Tom! Are you crazy? Like a fox! Oh, come on Dute! I would like to travel for a year, than we could buy a mobile home or something. Tom and Shirley did go to Montrose for a few months. They rented a campsite to park the RV. That October Tom and Shirley went to Massachusetts to visit Tammy and Linda.

They paid a full month's rent at the campsite and took off in their truck for Massachusetts. Dad, would you like to go to Plumb Island today? Sure, it is a good day to go fishing! I'm going to collect some shells. If you find any nice ones save some for me. Alright Dad, I know that you like Plumb Island. It is so peaceful here. I'm glad that I get you to myself for once. I love just being alone with you and talking to you Dad. I love you. While at the beach Linda ask her Dad if they were going to stay traveling or if they wanted to stay in Massachusetts. I think your Ma, ma wants to move back to New Jersey. I wish you would stay here. I love it here too.

Except Dute has her mind made up in living in New Jersey. She has done a lot for me in the past several years and now it is time for me to do what she wants me to do. I guess you are right Dad. You do need to slow down a little. Mom does need a stable environment! She has to take her medicine for her blood pressure and diabetes. You are both not that healthy and need to settle down. Tom and Shirley stayed with Tammy most of the winter.

January 2000: Tom and Shirley than went to New Jersey to visit with Thomas and Jackie. Dad, look at this Mobile home for sale. It is only five thousand dollars. Tom, we should check it out. Shirley called for an appointment. Tom we are going to see it in the morning. Thomas said well you know that this hotel is expensive! We charge by the hour, twenty five cents to use the bathroom one dollar for dinner and ten cents to read the news paper. Thomas, stop it! Be nice to your parents. Thomas just loves joking with people. They all laughed.

We are going to Salem tomorrow at one in the afternoon to see Mr. McCann. I'll go with you if want me too. That would be nice Thomas. Shirley said. The next morning Tom, Shirley and Thomas went to Salem a little early to see the mobile home. Hello, you must be Tom.

Yes and this is my wife Shirley and my son Thomas. This home has one bedroom. It is big enough for us. Tom and I are the only ones who will live here. Our kids are grown. How is the heater and the hot water heater? To be honest with you they are not that good.

They need work or to be replaced. That is alright, I am a plumber by trade. Well Tom we could make a deal if you want to fix any of the problems that you find. How about four thousand dollars? Tom that sounds reasonable? Are you willing to let us make payments? We could let you pay one hundred sixty one dollars a month as well as the lot rent of two seventy five. That sounds good to me. Well, Tom than its sold!

Shirley wrote out a check for the rent and the deposit and then ask when can we move in? As soon as you want too. Good, we wanted to move in yesterday. Tom and Shirley did move in the next week. Tom put in a new hot water heater and cleaned the heater and replaced the nozzle. The heater worked just after the cleaning. Dute, I am going to build on a porch so that I can do my crafts and smoke out there without getting wet or cold. I saw some windows for sale. What in the hell are you going to do with them? They won't fit our house. I told you Dute, I am going to build on a porch. I'll believe it when I see it. Thomas and Tom went to Lowes and bought some lumber and sheet rock. In the next few days Tom had built the porch as he said that he was going to build.

August 4, 2000. Hi mom who's there? Oh, its Thomas, Jackie. Terri, George and the kids. Were having a party for your Dad's birthday. Let me talk to Dad. Linda sounded very angry. I didn't know that you were having a party for Dad's birthday! I should have been invited! We thought you wouldn't come since you and Tammy live in Massachusetts. Well you act like we are not family. I really don't want to talk about this right now! Just let me talk to Dad. Tom it's Linda on the phone. Hello. Hello Dad. Happy sixty fifth birthday! I am going to take vacation at Christmas time and I will bring you your gift than. Too bad you couldn't come down for my party.

I would have come if I only knew about the party. I was not invited to your party. I'm sorry Linda; I guess that Thomas thought that you and Tammy wouldn't come to New Jersey right now. Well Dad that is awfully funny because I always come to New Jersey any other time. I always make a way to be with family. Well any way Dad have a happy birthday. I'll see you at Christmas for a week. I love you Dad. I love you too, see ya.

On that note Linda hung the phone feeling hurt and left out. Christmas day the Phillips house was full of family. Linda was thinking to herself, I don't think that I can stay here, I am so sick. Hi, Dad, Hi, Mom. I have to sit down. Linda what's wrong? I feel sick! I wasn't feeling good yesterday. I have been vomiting and sleeping all morning that is why I wasn't here sooner. I think I have the flu. I have a headache and I need to lay down. Go lay down on our bed. Mom I can't, I think I am going back to the motel room. I can't stand all of the cigarette smoke, it is making me sick. I'll try to come back to visit before I go home.

January 2, 2001: Hello Mom, I was trying to make it to your house before I went home Linda said on the phone. I know that you wanted to come back but obviously you were feeling sick. Some vacation that was. I can't believe that I had the flu at Christmas time. Tell Dad that I miss him and I hope to go to New Jersey soon. Linda, I have to hang up for now, I'm watching a movie. Bye Mom. Than Linda hung up the phone.

Chapter # 26

April 2001: Tammy, are you going to New Jersey for Moms sixty fifth birthday party? No I have to work. I'll be going on vacation in July. I'll get to see Mom and Dad than. Well I guess the kids and I be leaving on Friday morning. Alright Linda be careful on the roads. I will see you when you come home. Hi, Dad surprise! Linda, I didn't know that you were coming down. Is Tammy with you? No, she couldn't get the time off. She did tell me to tell you hello and that she will see you in July. Where is Mom? She is working at Sunoco part time, for extra money.

I'm glad that she's not here right now. I don't want to spoil her surprise party. What time does she finish work? She usually works until around ten p.m. Oh good! We have time to be alone to talk. Linda, take a look at this envelope. What is this suppose to be? It is the dream I had last night. Do you know where those two building are? Or what they are? They look like the world trade center buildings to me. That's exactly what I saw in my dream. Is this an airplane crashing through the building?

Yes, and just to let you know a few thousand people will die. This will be one of he most horrific scenes that the United States has ever seen! Dad, you are scaring me. Stop lying. Believe me I am not lying. I'm not exactly sure when this will happen but the emergency number kept flashing in my dream. You mean 911 Dad? Yes, I will not be here to see it. Stop acting crazy Dad! I am not crazy, just believe me.

You will see that not just one plane will cause trouble it will be several air planes taken by Hi-Jackers. This action will cause a war that will last at least ten years. People will lose their jobs, homes and will be hungry. This country will go into a financial tail spin. Just be prepared! Please, listen to me. Ok Dad, Linda said with doubt in her voice and thinking to herself, Dad is losing his mind. This is not the first time that I have had a dream that had come true. God has told me that this will not happen in my life time but it will be in yours. Dad, you need to stop! You are giving me goose bumps! I know you think I'm losing my mind, I only wish I were.

God does give some people the knowledge and power to see things others can't or won't see, or even use. Linda you do have the gift. Just let God show you the way. I guess I do see at times something's that we can't explain. Dad I do remember the day that Tammy and I were passing by Malden Mills in Methuen, Massachusetts and I said to Tammy if that place ever catches on fire it will burn to the ground. I could actually see the mill in flames!

Two weeks after I said that the Mill did burn down to the ground! I remember seeing the news that morning. I remember the first thing that I did was to scream and then I began to cry. Am I psychic? I don't know. Can we just change the subject? I guess I should go and take the kids some dinner back to the hotel. Don't tell Mom that I am here. I will see her tomorrow, and I will see you than Dad. Linda hugged Tom and kissed him on the cheek.

Hey Terri I'm here! What can I do to help you with for the party? There is not too much left to do? Would you like some soda? Of course I would. What did you get Mom for her birthday? I thought that it would be funny if I took sixty five ones and taped them together. Take half and make a six and than the other half and make a five. We could hang the six and the five on the wall as a decoration! Linda, where do you get this stuff from. I don't know Terri I guess I just make it up as I go along. Where is Mom going to sit? Right there in the rocking chair. It will be funny sixty five ones all taped up and Mom will go crazy taking them apart.

Shirley walked into Terri's house. Surprise everyone said. I knew it! Linda when did you get here? Yesterday, you mean to tell me that Dad didn't tell you I was here? No, when did you get here. Around noon yesterday. Where is Dad? He's outside talking to Ingrid and Rickey. (Josephine's Son and daughter- In - law) Well I'm going to see what Dad is up to. Hey Dad, I was wondering what you were doing.. I thought that I would get some fresh air and catch a smoke.

You know I can't sit in a stuffy house with stuffy people. Too many Norton's in one room. Tom cracked a smile. Dad you are too funny! They both were laughing now. I still have goose bumps about what we talked about last night. Well let me tell you something else. You know that baby in the stroller right there? Yes, It is Kathleen's daughter right? Yes but more than that Linda, that is my sister Eva. Of course I can't prove it now but watch when she grows up. I won't be around to see it but you will. What are you talking about Dad? There you go acting crazy again.

Believe me Linda that baby is my sister she has Eva's eyes! Dad I will talk to you later. I am going inside to tell Mom Happy Birthday. Mom do you want me to help you take those ones apart. If you want too Linda. Mom how do you like your dozen roses? I love them! I love the money too! How did you make the ones into the six and the five. I don't know Mom I just did. Well I really did like my party and my presents. I'm glad you could be here. Me too Mom.

When Linda went back outside Tom was still there on the porch. Dad I'm glad I had a chance to see you. I just wanted to say goodbye in person. Linda than hugged Tom and kissed him on the cheek. See Ya Dad, I'll miss you.

June 2001: Fathers Day. Hello, Mom is Dad there? Tom, it's for you, Linda is calling. Hi, Dad how are you doing? Ah, pretty good! Happy Fathers Day! Sorry I didn't send you a present yet. I have one for Mom for Mothers Day too. It's alright Linda, don't worry about it. I have plenty of presents. A man can only have so many pairs of sox, Tee shirts, and of under shorts. Well Dad I guess you really never need any of that kind of stuff! I was thinking about taking you and Mom out to the casino and dinner.

We will be able to do this when I come down in August. Oh, you will be here in August? Yes Dad around the twenty eighth. I get my vacation then. I think it will be nice to bring Monica and Jessica and let them unwind before the school year. Well that sounds good! Dad how is the weather in Jersey? It's great! Nice and sunny! We are having a cookout with Thomas and Jackie today. Are they there now? No, they are coming soon. It is raining it's ass off here! I am cooking out here on the balcony. I'm sitting out here watching it rain.

I have hamburgers and hot dogs on the grill. Linda, you do know that we've been on the phone a couple of hours now. Oh, Dad I don't care, you are my father and it's father's day! Than Tom said I want my cake! Quoting a line from Stephen Kings Creep Show. Wow, Dad do you hear that! It sounds like its raining buckets. Yea man it's really pouring now. Do you remember that pouring rain in the 1980s here In Massachusetts? I guess I do!

I was the one who had to clean out the bowling alley. There was about two feet of water in that bowling alley. Gee it's really pouring! You should see the trash floating by. The cars look like they are floating too. Linda and Tom laughed for a few minutes. Well, Dad I know that I've talked your ear off. I really can't help it. I really need to see you. Do you want to talk to your Mother? No Dad I'll call her later. Goodbye Dad, See ya later! Tom hung up his phone than Linda hung up her phone. That Fathers Day phone call lasted around three hours. In the next couple of weeks Linda called Tom many times. During this one particular phone call Tom told Linda about a poem that he wrote called The First Orchestra. Here is how it goes.

"The First Orchestra"

In the beginning of the very first day you would see the trees start to swing and sway. One by one by each bird took it's place. They landed on the limbs in style and grace. Each one as they landed would make a sound, all birds joined in even the ones on the ground, all the bird's tooted different the way they were dressed they had different sounds always did their best. One by one they started a tune, you couldn't tell what they were playing it was too soon, as I looked around the last ones flew in, some landed on the trees and some on the ground. One by one they started their favorite sounds, the birds in the trees all the ones on the ground to say the Orchestra was playing was the greatest thing to hear, they want all of us to live together and never be in fear. The next time you see birds on the ground or in a tree, you know they started the orchestra just for you and me, all the birds become quiet and I didn't know why they were looking up to the Director in the sky.

Written By,

Tom Phillips

Chapter #27

June 30th 2001: Hi Dad, I talked to Mom earlier, did she tell you that Jessica needs an operation? She said something about her gallbladder? Yes, Dad she had gallstones and her gallbladder is diseased. There is one thing bothering me though. What is wrong Linda? Well, Jessica told me on Friday when we went to the Doctors that she thinks she is going to die during surgery. I'm scared Dad! I mean really scared! She even described the type of casket that she wants. She says it should be white with red roses. She also told me not to cry because god needs her. Dad she is only twelve years old. No, Linda she is wrong. She is not going to die!

I'll be sure to take care of that. What do you mean about that? I can't tell you, I just will! I had a dream but god won't let me give you any of the details. Linda thought to herself, there you go again, acting crazy. Linda I will pray to God to take care of everything. I am praying too…Linda let me talk to Jessica now. Ok, Dad. I love you, see you soon. Jessica Pop Pop wants to talk to you.

Hi Pop Pop how are you? I'm doing fine baby, how are you? I need an operation Pop Pop and I'm scared. I think I'm going to die. No you are not going to die. Pop Pop is taking care of everything. Don't forget that I love you baby! I love you too Pop Pop, goodbye! Jessica where is my Dad, the phone went dead. He said goodbye and then he hung up.

Well I guess I'll call him later or tomorrow. Linda had felt like calling her father back but thought I'll just call him on Monday or Tuesday.

Monday evening, I think I'll call to New Jersey to see what Mom and Dad are doing. No maybe I'll wait until Tuesday or Wednesday. Mom, you know that Aunt Tammy is visiting Mom Mom and Pop Pop. I guess it would be best if I wait until than. Tammy needs to spend some time with Mom and Dad.

July 3, 2001: MOM, its Uncle Thomas! There has been an emergency! In a chocking voice Thomas said, Dad died! What did you say? I said Dad died! Speak English! Speak English! Linda, get a hold of yourself and listen! Ok Thomas, are you telling me that Dad is dead? How? Why? Linda began to cry, Noooo!!! Are you coming down to New Jersey? Yes, Thomas I will be on the road as soon as I can get myself together. I will be there!

Tom died on Tuesday July third and he was buried on Saturday July the seventh two thousand and one. I know all about this because I am Tom's Daughter, Linda Jean Phillips Santiago. I often wonder how I can live without my father, my friend and most of all my Hero! I will Miss You DAD!!!

In conclusion, The one thing that I have realized through all of the pain and heartache is that life does go on and the memories and love my father gave to me, my brother and my three sisters and of course the love of his life my Mom, Shirley (Dute) Phillips, will last forever!

The End
Linda Jean Santiago